AF142085

Rahel Rüth

THE INFLUENCE OF TRUST ON LEADER-MEMBER EXCHANGE IN CULTURALLY DIVERSE LEADER-MEMBER DYADS

Rahel Rüth

THE INFLUENCE OF TRUST ON LEADER-MEMBER EXCHANGE IN CULTURALLY DIVERSE LEADER-MEMBER DYADS

WFA MEDIEN VERLAG

Bibliografische Information der Deutschen Nationalbibliothek
Die Deutsche Nationalbibliothek verzeichnet diese Publikation in der Deutschen Nationalbibliografie; detaillierte bibliografische Daten sind im Internet über http://dnb.dnb.de abrufbar.

ISBN Paperback: 978-3-946589-00-6
ISBN Hardcover: 978-3-946589-01-3
ISBN E-Book: 978-3-946589-02-0

© WFA Medien Verlag, Stuttgart
WFA Medien Verlag | Patrick Haag, Uhlandstr. 65, 71299 Wimsheim

Das Werk einschließlich aller seiner Teile ist urheberrechtlich geschützt. Jede Verwertung, die nicht ausdrücklich vom Urheberrechtsgesetz zugelassen ist, bedarf der vorherigen Zustimmung des Verlags. Das gilt insbesondere für Vervielfältigungen, Bearbeitungen, Übersetzungen, Mikroverfilmungen und die Einspeicherung und Verarbeitung in elektronischen Systemen.

Die Wiedergabe von Gebrauchsnamen, Handelsnamen, Warenbezeichnungen usw. in diesem Werk berechtigt auch ohne besondere Kennzeichnung nicht zu der Annahme, dass solche Namen im Sinne der Warenzeichen- und Markenschutz-Gesetzgebung als frei zu betrachten wären und daher von jedermann benutzt werden dürften.

www.wfa-medien-verlag.de

I Abstract

Due to the increased need of multinational companies to manage business activities abroad, this study examines the influence of trust on culturally diverse Leader-Member Dyads. By interviewing both leaders and members of nine German-Chinese dyads employed in German multinational enterprises in mainland China, the study finds that trust is a necessary precondition for establishing high-quality exchange between culturally diverse co-workers. However, quality of exchange is valued differently across cultures. Moreover, cultural and linguistic hindrances to the formation of trust particular to the German-Chinese context are identified. After having established a trustful relationship, co-workers can capitalize on the cultural diversity of their partner in order to accomplish common objectives and increase work efficiency. It is finally found, that a process of cultural approximation exists, that simplifies the formation of trust and high-quality Leader-Member Exchange (LMX).

Findings contribute to LMX theory by putting culturally diverse Leader-Member Dyads to the focus of attention. Furthermore they extend upon culture specific management and leadership research by highlighting differences inherent to German and Chinese management practices.

II Table of Contents

III   Table of Figures

IV Table of Abbreviations

ALS	-	Average Leadership Style
CBT	-	Calculus-Based Trust
EU	-	European Union
FDI	-	Foreign Direct Investment
GDP	-	Gross Domestic Product
H-I	-	Horizontal-Individualist
IBT	-	Identification-Based Trust
LM-Dyad	-	Leader Member Dyad
LMX	-	Leader-Member Exchange
MNC	-	Multinational Company
MNE	-	Multinational Enterprise
MNT	-	Multinational Team
PPP	-	Purchasing Power Parity
PRC	-	People's Republic of China
SET	-	Social Exchange Theory
US	-	United States
USA	-	United States of America
V-C	-	Vertical-Collectivist
VDL	-	Vertical Dyad Linkage
WVS	-	World Values Survey

1   Introduction

"To an ever-increasing extent, 'work' involves close interaction and cooperation with people who come from a national-societal cultural background different from one's own". Ferrin and Gillespie (2010, p. 42) trace this emerging condition back to an increasingly globalized world, in which multinational enterprises (MNE) operate on intertwined international markets, occupy a culturally diverse workforce and due to the rise of new communication technologies consider it a matter of course to work in global virtual teams (Ferrin & Gillespie, 2010). Along with the relentless advance of globalization and its worldwide consequences, managers and employees are increasingly confronted with the challenge of managing "unfamiliar relationships with unfamiliar parties" (Saunders et al., 2010, p. i).

It was in the early 1970s that Graen and colleagues introduced a new approach to leadership in organizations (e.g. Graen et al., 1972; Dansereau et al., 1975), claiming that "leadership can only occur in the vertical dyad" (Dansereau et al., 1975, p. 76). By shifting the focus of leadership research on the dyadic work relationship between a superior leader and a subordinate member, Graen and fellow scholars enabled management researchers to take a closer look at how leadership dynamics evolve in particular work relationships. The focus on dyadic relationships between a superior and a subordinate proved to become the cornerstone of modern-day Leader-Member Exchange (LMX) theory, a construct that measures the quality of the exchange between leader and member in a vertical dyad.

In a globalized and interrelated world however, LMX theory needs to keep pace and evolve along with the changing realities of our time. When work involves the interaction and cooperation with people from diverse cultural backgrounds, LMX theory needs to put focus on the dyadic work relationships between leaders and members from different cultures. Following the dyadic leadership approach, it is thus the aim of this study to contribute to the challenges modern-day management is facing in a globalized world.

Researchers have indeed dealt extensively with LMX theory ever since it's introduction, and scholars have acknowledged the importance of integrating the construct of culture with LMX (Hiller & Day, 2003). However, even though integrating the component of culture to their research, the vast majority of studies addresses LMX in LM-Dyads to which both partners bring the same cultural background, while no influential works focusing on culturally diverse LM-Dyads can be detected. Scandura and Lankau (1996) noted the absence of LMX research focused on culturally diverse LM-Dyads early on and called for research directed to this niche. However, their call remained largely unheard, which is why a research gap is evolving that this study is aiming to address.

Since trust is described as being "essential for stable social relationships" (Blau, 1964, p. 99), the concept takes a prominent place in LMX literature. Scholars agree that trust positively influences LMX (e.g. Gómez & Rosen, 2001; Dirks & Ferrin, 2001; Ferris et al., 2009), but debate lengthily over the exact nature of the relationship (Scandura & Pelligrini, 2008). The element of trust has even been considered in studies addressing LMX in a cross-cultural context (e.g. Dulebohn et al., 2012; Rockstuhl et al., 2012), but although a clear connection is drawn between trust and LMX in an intercultural context, focus is continuously laid on mono-cultural LM-Dyads.

By aiming at addressing the emergent research gap, this study puts focus on two specific cultural backgrounds, namely that of the People's Republic of China (PRC) and that of Federal Republic of Germany. The economy of the PRC has gained significant importance during the last two decades, evolving from a third world country to one of the world's most powerful economies of the 21st century (IMF, 2015). It is tied to Germany by strong economic bonds, mutual trade and a considerable amount of reciprocal FDI (Foreign Direct Investment) (OECD, 2014). From a managerial point of view China and Germany therefore represent an interesting example for the challenges of modern-day management. However, from a researcher's point of view the opposing cultural backgrounds of the two countries in various cultural classifications (e.g. Hofstede, 1980, Triandis, 1995, Hall, 1976) render the two distinct cultural contexts even more promising as object of research.

By qualitatively interviewing leaders and members of nine German-Chinese Leader-Member Dyads (LM-Dyads), all of them employed in German MNEs but stationed in Mainland China, this study is examining how trust is built up between them and how it influences the quality of their exchange. It is thereby answering the need of both Chinese and German managers to understand their partners' leadership practices and to establish efficient work relationships with them. Furthermore in concentrating research on culturally diverse LM-Dyads, the study addresses the identified research gap. Thereby the main focus of interest always lies on the importance of trust for cross-cultural LMX. The study addresses the importance of trust for both members of culturally diverse LM-Dyads, questioning whether differences can be detected across cultures. Hereby the process of trust formation and the generation of high-quality LMX across cultures are highlighted further. Finally the process of cultural approximation is investigated and conclusions on its relevance for LMX in culturally diverse LM-Dyads are drawn.

In order to address the research objectives, first a comprehensive literature review is conducted, thus providing a theoretical framework for the study. In a second step the applied methodology is presented and the choice of the research setting thereby explained in depth. Findings are derived subsequently, followed by a discussion that puts them in the perspective of existent theories. Finally managerial implications will be summarized and limitations of the study outlined.

2 Theoretical Framework

The following section gives an overview of the development and current state of research in LMX and trust literature, presenting seminal works, pointing out central debates and explaining important concepts. Established links between both areas are pointed out and tied to findings of the field of intercultural studies. By contrasting the concepts' state of research in a German and a Chinese context the starting point for further research is identified and the research questions of the study derived.

2.1 LMX Theory: Evolution and Conceptual Discrepancies

In 1972 Graen and colleagues first directed the attention of the field of leadership research to the dyadic work relationship between supervisors (leaders) and their subordinates (members). They argued that an Average Leadership Style (ALS), which is the general leadership style of a supervisor towards the group of his subordinates, could not sufficiently explain variations in leader behavior. Building on their observations, Danserau and colleagues (1973) proposed the Vertical Dyad Linkage (VDL) model, thus shifting focus from the behavior of a leader towards his "members-in-general" (Dansereau et al., 1973, p. 187), to the behavior of a leader towards a member-in-particular. The concept stresses that the individual personality and situation of members significantly influences the relationship between leader and member. From then on the particular relationships between a leader and each of his assigned members became the basic unit of analysis. The vertical dyad is thereby composed of three defining elements: First, a superior, second, a subordinate and third, a set of exchange relationships between the two (Graen et al., 1977). Focusing on the latter, VDL theory was developed further and emerged to be known as "Leader-Member Exchange" (LMX) theory (Graen & Cashman, 1975). As LMX literature thus studies the exchange relationship between leader and member, the theory is rooted in Social Exchange Theory (SET) (Settoon et al., 1996), which examines social exchanges in various contexts.

Although much research has been conducted on LMX since the construct's development in the 1970s (Graen & Uhl-Bien, 1995; Rockstuhl et al., 2012), scholars criticize that little theorizing groundwork has been presented, research has not been consolidated and literature is discordant even about the construct's basic definition (Schriesheim et al., 1999). However, the majority of studies on LMX agree that the nature of the construct can be described as the quality of the exchange relationship between supervisors and subordinates (Graen & Scandura, 1987; Schriesheim et al., 1999). Furthermore, consistency among researchers is found in the construct's basic assumptions. As the theory is rooted in SET, scholars agree that the interactions between leaders and members are interdependent and contingent on the actions of the respective partner (Blau, 1964; Cropanzo & Mitchell, 2005). This implicates that LMX can be measured along a continuum reaching from high-quality exchange towards low-quality exchange (Dienesch & Liden, 1986). High-quality exchange is thereby marked by feelings of mutual obligation and reciprocity (Gouldner, 1960; Liden et al., 1997) whereas low-quality relationships are defined by a mere economic, formally agreed upon exchange (Blau, 1964). Although researchers agree that high-quality LMX contains reciprocity (Brower et al., 2000), this reciprocity is not necessarily a balanced one. Research states that the assessment of LMX quality can vary between members of a LM-Dyad, with one partner rating it very high while the other partner is considering it to be low (Gerstner & Day, 1997).

Due to discrepancies in the conceptualization, the measurement of LMX remains inconsistent as well. Various scales were proposed, with most of them lacking proper justification by their authors (Schriesheim et al., 1999). Furthermore, scholars question the emergence of a one-dimensional LMX construct (ibid.), suggesting that in line with its theoretical underpinnings of SET, LMX was much more to be seen as a multidimensional construct (Dienesch & Liden, 1986, Liden et al., 1997).

Dienesch and Liden (1986) suggested a three-dimensional model of LMX, proposing the dimensions of "Contribution", "Loyalty" and "Affect" (Dienesch & Liden, 1986, pp. 624). Their approach was validated in various quantitative studies (e.g. Phillips et al., 1993; Liden & Maslyn, 1998; Greguras & Ford, 2006) and further enhanced by Liden and Maslyn (1998), who built upon their dimensions and identified an additional one: "Professional Respect". The dimension of Contribution thereby points to the respective efforts each co-worker contributes in order to reach the mutual goals of the dyad. Loyalty is the public support for the co-worker and his or her goals, Affect relates to the mutual liking both co-workers have for each other and Professional Respect means the perception of the partner's excellence in his or her work. Although later studies identified additional dimensions (Schriesheim et al., 1999; Brower et al., 2000), the proposal of Liden and Maslyn (1998) has been widely accepted as the conceptual basis of multidimensionality in LMX research (Schriesheim et al, 1999; Greguras & Ford, 2006).

However, discordance among scholars and conceptual ambiguity of the construct reaches even further. Scholars have tested various antecedents and consequences of LMX, with no one aiming at inductively deriving a complete set that would contribute to the theorizing groundwork of the LMX construct. Thus, tested antecedents as well as outcomes are manifold but seemingly unstructured. Brower and colleagues (2000) even point out that the dimensions identified earlier by Liden and Maslyn (1998) could as well be interpreted as antecedents of LMX, as none of them is a necessary condition for LMX but they rather "contribute to the level of LMX in an additive fashion" (Brower et al., 2000, p. 235). Dulebohn and colleagues (2012) realized the absence of a comprehensive empirical examination of antecedents and outcomes of LMX and in addressing the research gap conducted a meta-analysis, uniting 247 studies, examining 21 distinct antecedents and 16 consequences of high-quality LMX. Furthermore they tested 4 moderators on the relationship of antecedents and LMX. Their findings implicated that leader variables account for the largest variances in the quality of a LM-Dyad's exchange, implicating that a leader is dominant in influencing the LMX quality of the LM-Dyad (Dienesch & Liden, 1986). Interestingly, they also found out that moderators such as the scale of LMX applied throughout prior studies do not bias the findings. The sheer amount of independent antecedents and outcomes Dulebohn and colleagues (2012) identified throughout LMX literature illustrates how dispersed research in the field still is. Although they made a significant contribution to the field of LMX theory, there is still a shortage of theorizing groundwork. No inductive and comprehensive study of antecedents, outcomes or dimensions of LMX has been conducted, resulting in a dispersed theory that is in need for an ongoing process of consolidation.

2.2   Trust: Models and Forms

While making the point that "trust is essential for understanding interpersonal and group behavior, managerial effectiveness, economic exchange and social or political stability" (Hosmer, 1995, p. 379) and thus acknowledging the importance of the concept for leadership research, Hosmer also notes that a number of differing definitions of trust have been proposed. In the field of organizational studies the conceptual work of Mayer, Davis and Schoorman (1995) has gained significant recognition as seminal study (Rousseau, 1998) and according to scientific search engines was cited more than 12,000 times (Google Scholar, October 2nd, 2015) in subsequent studies. In their work, trust is defined as "the willingness of a party to be vulnerable to the actions of another party based on the expectation that the other will perform a particular action important to the trustor, irrespective of the ability to monitor or control that other party" (Mayer et al., 1995, p. 712). Besides proposing a definition of trust that came to be widely accepted among scholars in the field of organizational studies, Mayer and colleagues (1995) also conceptualized a model of trust, that integrates antecedents and outcomes of the concept respectively and is depicted in Figure 1. For them, a trustee has to show three distinct but correlated factors of perceived trustworthiness: Ability, which is a "group of skills, competencies and characteristics that enable a party to have influence within a specific domain" (Mayer et al., 1995, p. 717), Benevolence, meaning the "extent to which a trustee is believed to want to do good to the trustor" (ibid., p. 718), and finally, Integrity, defined as "the trustor's perception that the trustee adheres to a set of principles that the trustor finds acceptable" (ibid., p. 719). In addition to the three factors of perceived trustworthiness, the emergence of trust is further contingent on the trustor's propensity to trust. Mayer and colleagues (1995) argue, that each person is different in their inherent willingness to trust others without disposing of data on the other party. Thus the inherent propensity to trust is decisive for the likelihood that one party will develop trust towards the other (Mayer et al., 1995).

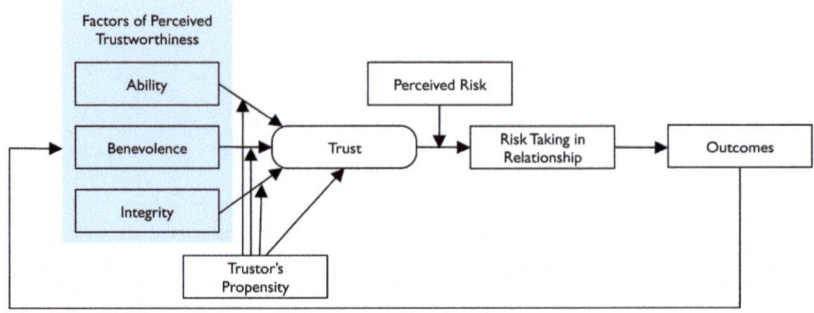

Figure 1: Integrative Model of Trust
(Own Depiction after Mayer et al., 1995, p. 715)

Building on Mayer and colleagues' definition of trust, Colquitt and colleagues (2007) conducted a meta-analysis on trust, trustworthiness and propensity to trust. They stress that two primary components are decisive for trust to build up. The first of them is the intention of the trustee to accept vulnerability, whereas the second is the trustor's positive expectations in the respective trustee.

Many more scholars subsequently expanded upon Mayer and colleagues' framework, recognizing its significance for the field of management studies (Serva et al., 2005). In an attempt to broaden the concept, researchers have dealt either with trust building in a specific phase (Rousseau et al., 1998; McKnight et al., 1998) or examined its influences on different levels of analysis, thus shifting the original model's focus from the interpersonal relationship between two parties to an organizational level of analysis (Schoorman et al., 2007). However, as this study is focusing on trust in dyadic work relationships, findings on other than the dyadic level of organizing are not of direct relevance for the further development of reasoning.

Deriving their insight from the works of Lewicki and colleagues (1998) as well as Sitkin and Roth (1993), Rousseau and colleagues (1998) state further that trust has a "bandwidth" (Rousseau et al., 1998, p. 398). According to the authors and as illustrated in Figure 2, trust can vary along a scope that reaches from Calculus-Based Trust (CBT) in an early stage of relationship development to Identification-Based Trust (IBT) in later stages, depending on the history of the two involved parties' relationship, the stage of the relationship's development and cues in the immediate setting. Calculus-Based Trust is built on a market-oriented, transactional calculation that economically weighs the positive outcomes from sustaining a relationship against the costs of forfeiting it (Lewicki & Bunker, 1995). Thus CBT is a "partial and fragile" form of trust (Scandura & Pelligirini, 2008, p. 103), located at the lower end of the scope. Opposed to CBT, Identification-Based Trust is based on reciprocal affect and concern of the parties involved in the relationship (McAllister, 1995). IBT therefore "allows the members to be confident that their interests will be fully protected and that no surveillance of the other member is necessary" (Scandura & Pelligrini, 2008, p. 104).

Rousseau and colleagues (1998) propose an additional form of trust, Institution-Based Trust, although scholars are discordant on whether it is a form of trust or merely a form of control. Institution-Based Trust is built upon the existence of institutional factors in the surrounding environment such as society or an organizational setting that can support further risk taking and trust behaviors (Sitkin, 1995). As Institution-Based Trust is based on external factors, it does not need time to develop and is thus located at the early end of the trust scope.

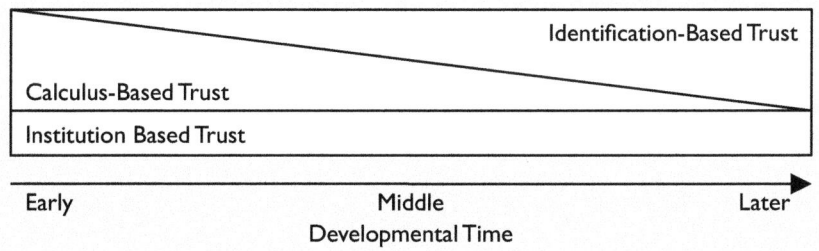

Figure 2: Different Forms of Trust
(Own Depiction after Rousseau et al., 1998, p. 401)

Differentiating between differing forms of trust can help to classify trusting relationships. It is therefore considered an important finding for the development of this study.

2.3 Culture: Comparability Along Dimensions

"As globalization continues to spread throughout the world, issues of diversity and cross-cultural leadership take on new importance. Global enterprise demands that leaders and managers be responsive to the practices, norms and values of their foreign business partners" (Sullivan et al., 2003, p. 184). Culture is thus becoming an element that can no longer be neglected in modern day leadership theory.

Groundbreaking works aiming at making cultures comprehensible and comparative date back to 1961, when Kluckhohn and Strodtbeck first postulated that cultures are exhibiting constant "orientations" towards the world and other people, and can thus be measured in terms of those value orientations. Another early scholar was Hall (1976), who, coming from the field of anthropology, distinguishes between high-context and low-context cultures that are located at opposite ends of a continuum. In his framework members of high-context cultures depend heavily on the interpretation of implicit clues, rooted in their shared experiences and cultural environment when engaging in communication, whereas members of low-context cultures value explicit language (Hall, 1976, p. 91; Mead & Andrews, 2009, pp. 33f.).

The most influential scholar in the field of cultural research to date remains Geert Hofstede (1980), who powerfully directed management scholars' attention towards the subject (Trompenaars & Hampden-Turner, 1997, p. x). In his study of 53 nations, Hofstede inductively derived an originally four-dimensional framework of culture, thereby defining the term as "the collective programming of the mind, that distinguishes the members of one group or category of people from another" (Hofestede, 2001, p. 9). According to his results, culture can be measured along the dimensions of Power Distance, Uncertainty Avoidance, Individualism as opposed to Collectivism, and Masculinity as opposed to Femininity. Power Distance hereby relates to the degree to which the members of a certain culture accept inequality (Cullen & Parboteeah, 2014, p. 69). Uncertainty Avoidance is defined as "the extent to which the members of a culture feel threatened by uncertain or unknown situations" (Hofstede, 2001, p. 161). The continuum of Individualism versus Collectivism takes into account the identity of people as individuals, opposed to their relation to a group in society (Niles, 1998). Hofstede defines an individualistic society as one "in which the ties between individuals are loose" (Hofstede, 2001, p. 225), where "everyone is expected to look after him/herself and her/his immediate family only" (ibid.), whereas a collectivistic society is one "in which people from birth onwards are integrated into strong, cohesive in-groups, which throughout people's lifetime continue to protect them in exchange for unquestioning loyalty" (ibid). Finally, masculinity addresses the attitude of a society towards traditional gender roles. Whereas cultures high on the masculinity index value traditionally masculine behaviors such as Machismo, cultures positioned low on the masculinity index are marked by blurred gender roles, so that it is not unusual for men to behave expressive and affectionate (Johnson & Cullen, 2002). Two dimensions were added to Hofstede's original construct. Long-term Orientation as opposed to Short-term Orientation relates to the people's propensity to foster "virtues oriented towards future rewards" (Hofstede, 2001, p. 359). The dimension of Indulgence was the last one to be added to Hofstede's conceptualization, addressing the extent to which members of a society control their impulses and desires (Itim International, 2015). The accomplished comparability between cultures is among the major advantages of Hofstede's framework, enabling intercultural management to respond specifically to challenges posed by a foreign environment (Mead & Andrews, 2009, p. 44).

Although Hofstede's work is widely considered as seminal (Mead & Andrews, 2009, p. 29), other scholars such as Trompenaars (1993), Schwartz (1994) or House and colleagues (2004), to name only the most influential ones, have introduced differing or refined frameworks to classify culture. While the detailed structures of their approaches are not considered essential for the understanding of this study, one common trait is worth mentioning. Niles (1998) noted that the dimension of Individualism as opposed to Collectivism has been studied extensively among cultural researchers. Indeed the majority of frameworks mentioned above addresses the construct and integrates it into their theoretical approach toward culture. Singelis and colleagues state that "for cultures, individualism versus collectivism is the broadest division" (Singelis, Triandis et al., 1995, p. 243).

Building on that finding, Triandis (1995) classifies cultures into four categories. First, as considered the most basic distinction, he distinguishes collectivist and individualist cultures, whereas collectivists "define themselves as parts or aspects of a group" while "individualists focus on self-concepts that are autonomous from groups" (Singelis, Triandis et al., 1995, p. 243). The main defining and contrasting attribute between the two groups of people is thus the distinction between an interdependent and an independent self (Markus & Kitayama, 1991). Subsequently and in need to further specify those broad categories of culture Triandis (1995) made a distinction between vertical and horizontal individualism and collectivism, thereby focusing on the acceptance of inequality among a culture (Singelis, Triandis et al., 1995). For example, members postulating an autonomous self while feeling equal in status with other members of the society mark a horizontal-individualist (H-I) culture. In a vertical-collectivist (V-C) culture, the individual finds identity in a group whereas members of the in-group differ in status.

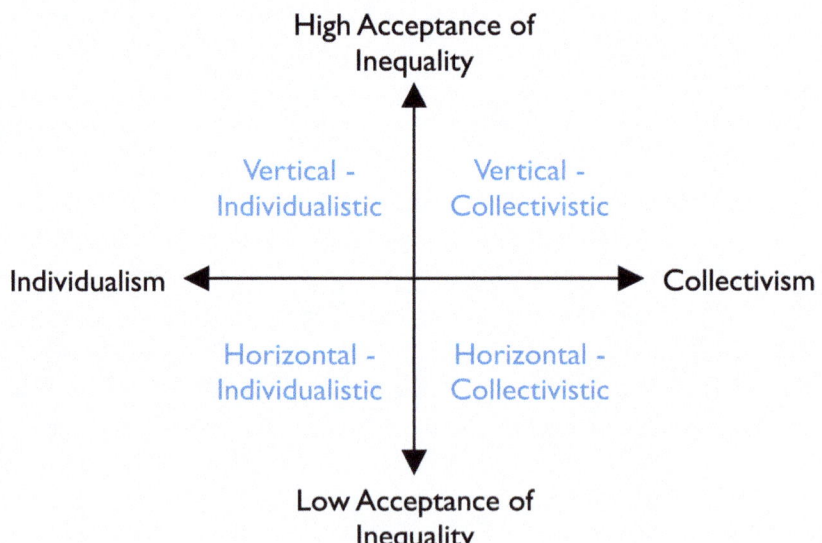

Figure 3: Classification of Culture According to Triandis

As illustrated in Figure 3, Triandis has thus developed a framework in which cultures can be classified along two dimensions, both drawing heavily upon Hofstede's dimensions of Individualism as opposed to Collectivism and Power Distance. Later researchers have frequently used the Triandis-framework to broadly categorize and distinguish cultures as it is backed by solid research, widely accepted and easy to apply. It is interesting however, that although equal in the definition of their dimensions or categories respectively, the different approaches of Triandis and Hofstede do not always yield congruent classifications of a culture. Whereas Triandis' findings clearly state that the US-American and Western European cultures are to be categorized as vertical-individualist (Singelis, Triandis et al., 1995), Hofstede's findings report low Power Distance for the US (40) as well as for parts of Western Europe (e.g. Germany 35), thus classifying them as horizontal-individualist (Itim International, 2015). However, as Triandis clarifies that Scandinavian Cultures are to be categorized as horizontal-indvidualist, it becomes clear that these countries are even lower on Hofstede's dimension on Power Distance (Sweden = 31; Denmark = 18; Norway = 31; Finland = 33)[1]. The question is thus where to draw the line between horizontal and vertical cultures on Hofstede's dimension of Power Distance. As researchers in the field of diversity and intercultural studies commonly classify Western cultures as horizontal-individualist (e.g. Rockstuhl et al., 2012; Dulebohn et al., 2012) and Hofstede's results also backen this approach for the US and Germany, this study will follow their example and categorize Western cultures as horizontal-individual, contrasting them to East-Asian vertical-collectivist societies.

---

1   France (68), Spain (57) and Italy (50) are rather high in Power Distance, whereas Austria (11), Switzerland (34) and the UK (35) are again rather low. These examples emphasize that „Western Europe" cannot be treated as a homogeneous cultural area, but rather diversity has to be acknowledged.

2.4 Integration: How the Concepts of LMX, Trust and Culture Relate

The constructs of LMX, trust and culture as presented and discussed in the previous paragraphs look back on a long tradition of research. As in a globalized world all three constructs are interrelated, various scholars have noticed the importance of integrating the approaches along the way (e.g. Fukuyama 1995; Zaheer & Zaheer, 2006; Schoorman et al., 2007). In order to provide a structured overview of the progress in the models' integration, first the main streams of research concerning the relationship between trust and LMX are presented, followed by an introduction of culture to the emergent findings.

2.4.1 LMX and Trust

In his landmark study of social exchange first published in 1964, Peter M. Blau describes trust as being "essential for stable social relationships" (p. 99). With LMX focusing on social exchange in LM-Dyads, trust consequently is an element that strongly relates. Ferris and colleagues' (2009) literature review on different kinds of working relationships accordingly illustrates that the single dimension of trust is considered vital for every specific working relationship they identified as being examined in literature.

Although LMX scholars widely agree that the constructs of trust and LMX are interrelated (e.g. Gómez & Rosen, 2001; Dirks & Ferrin, 2001), they are discordant on whether trust is to be seen as an antecedent or an outcome of LMX (Scandura & Pelligrini, 2008), with some researchers viewing trust also as a mere moderator variable (e.g. Sue-Chan et al., 2012; Dirks & Ferrin, 2001). Exemplary for the lack of agreement among researchers about the role of trust is the seminal work of Liden and Maslyn (1998) who extended upon Dienesch & Liden's (1986) approach to view LMX as a multidimensional construct. The authors explore whether trust is to be treated as a distinct dimension of LMX, concluding though that it is too close to the established dimension of loyalty to be distinguished. Instead, they redefine the loyalty dimension to explicitly include notions of trust into it. Throughout the course of LMX research, trust has thus been considered an antecedent of the construct, an outcome, a dimension and a moderator variable between LMX and various outcomes or antecedents. Researchers agree that an association is evident, but disagree on the nature of it (Scandura & Pelligrini, 2008).

Various scholars have furthermore attempted to integrate the constructs of LMX and trust. Among the first to conduct such an undertaking were Brower and colleagues (2000) who developed a "Model of Relational Leadership", building directly on Mayer and colleagues' (1995) work as shown in Figure 4. By differentiating between the trust of the leader towards the subordinate and vice versa, they developed a model that provides insights into the dynamics of the exchange relationship, illustrating how it is built iteratively.

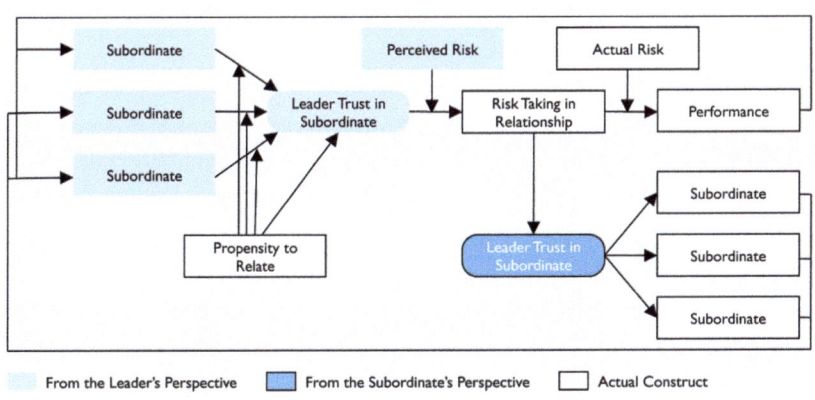

Figure 4: Model of Relational Leadership
(Own Depiction after Brower et al., 2000, p. 233)

Another attempt to integrate the literature on organizational trust and LMX was presented by Scandura and Pelligrini (2008). While not merging the constructs into a single new model, they distinguish between Calculus-Based Trust and Identification-Based Trust, relating both forms of trust separately to the quality of LMX. Neglecting the debate over the exact role of trust within the LMX framework, they find that LMX is positively related to both forms of trust. However, while the connection between IBT and LMX is positively linear, CBT is found to have a nonlinear association to trust. Economic balancing of costs and benefits to foster a high-quality LMX relationship can therefore prevail throughout the development of the exchange relationship. Scandura and Pelligrini's work demonstrates that CBT is found also in high-quality LMX relationships, thus highlighting their vulnerability to trust violations at any stage.

A further longitudinal study that examines the association between trust and LMX quality was conducted by Sue-Chan and colleagues in 2012. The authors similarly detect a positive association between trust and LMX by distinguishing however between leader trust in his subordinate and subordinate trust in his leader, thereby agreeing with Brower and colleagues (2000). They go as far as naming trust a "necessary precondition for entering into and developing a high-quality dyadic relationship" (Sue-Chan et al., 2012, p. 459).

2.4.2 The Component of Culture

"The word 'globalization' was not talked about 10 years ago. I could pick up books, business books, and it wasn't even in the index. It was nowhere to be found. Now it's become extremely important, almost to the point of being cliché" (Bingham et al., 2000, p. 291). John Pepper, former CEO and Chairman of Procter & Gamble, uttered this statement in the awareness that culture has become a factor that can no longer be ignored in leadership and management theory (as well as in reality). When thus discussing the concepts of LMX and dyadic trust in working relationships, the component of culture needs to be taken into account in order to keep pace with the emergent realities of our time.

The concept of trust is discussed controversially in the light of culture. Researchers debate whether to view trust as an etic concept, that is a universally consistent and applicable model, or as emic concept, meaning that people from different cultures interpret and therefore also enact trust differently (Dietz et al., 2010). Zaheer and Zaheer (2006) state that the etic view on trust is predominant in literature, thus it is constantly assumed that the understanding of trust through a Western lens is applicable for the study of trust among differing national contexts. This approach however is strongly criticized by Noorderhaven (1999), who argues that it is more effective to compare trust as well as its antecedents and consequences across different societies. An emic perspective on trust seems to be more fit to address the concept of trust in different cultural contexts (Lane, 1997). As the comprehensive model of Mayer and colleagues (1995) presented in Chapter 2.2 pursues an etic view, its implications have to be taken with care when applied to a cross-cultural context. In fact Zaheer and Zaheer (2006) along with Dietz and colleagues (2010) go even further and call for an integrated emic/etic approach, arguing that a such would yield insights into the different components of trust across nations while at the same time allow for comparison.

Apart from the discussion on whether trust is to be viewed as an etic or emic concept, researchers widely agree that societal norms and values influence the way trust is formed (Doney et al., 1998). Scholars further agree that the belonging to a certain culture influences a person's propensity to trust (Fukuyama, 1995; Lane, 1998). However, research has given opposing evidence concerning the direction of culture's influence on trust (Johnson & Cullen, 2002). It seems intuitive that members of collectivistic cultures are programmed on a higher propensity to trust than members of individualist cultures, as they develop strong in-group ties and view their self in relation to others. Although this notion has been confirmed by a number of studies and data (e.g. Doney et al., 1998; Hemesath & Pomponio, 1998; Johnson and Cullen, 2002), it is not commonly agreed upon amongst scholars. In fact a majority of researchers have adopted the opposite approach, arguing that members of individualist cultures display a generally larger propensity to trust. Evidence supports their notion (e.g. Kim & Son, 1998; Dulebohn et al., 2012). However, by comparing data from the World Values Survey (WVS), Johnson and Cullen (2002) remark that results cannot be generalized for cultural clusters such as the horizontal-individualist or the vertical-collectivist.

It is further of interest to point out that culture acts upon all forms of trust presented in Chapter 2.2 (Chen et al., 1998; Ferrin & Gillespie, 2010). Chen and colleagues (1998) argue that CBT is of greater importance in individualist cultures, whereas IBT is valued more in collectivist cultures as in-group relationships are marked by "communal sharing and emotional closeness" (Chen et al., 1998, p. 294). In their study the authors especially address trust development in working relationships. Finally, various scholars address the influence of culture on Institution-Based Trust (e.g. Johnson & Cullen, 2002; Coleman, 1990). Johnson and Cullen (2002, p. 354) thereby argue that especially "social institutions generally arise to facilitate trust". An example is the "Shame-Culture" predominant in

Asian collectivist societies that punishes wrongdoing by putting shame upon the offender and thus acts as moral safeguard (Heyer-Young, 2005, p. 182).

While the influence of culture on trust has been studied extensively, less albeit not few scholars have made an attempt to view the construct of LMX through a cultural lens. However, scholars have raised concerns about the validity of the concept in cultures other than the Western H-I culture in which it was originally conceptualized (Law et al., 2000, Anand et al., 2011). Hofstede dedicates an article to "cultural constraints in management theories" (Hofstede, 1993, p. 81), illustrating along the example of Alice in Wonderland how different rules apply in different cultures. Cultural context can thus render the concepts developed in one cultural sphere null and void in another.

This being said, researchers have pursued two broad, differing approaches to integrate the concept of culture with LMX (Anand et al., 2011). The first group of scholars has thereby attempted to transfer and apply LMX theory to specific cultural contexts (e.g. Aryee & Chen, 2006; Varma et al., 2005). In contrast, the second group concentrated their efforts on examining the relationship between different dimensions of culture and LMX in general, thus creating a framework applicable to various cultures along their measurable dimensions (e.g. Sullivan et al., 2003; Schaubroeck & Lam, 2002). The first approach is very specific and will thus be discussed for the two examples of Germany and China in the next paragraph. Findings of the second approach are as well widespread as researchers examined culture along differing dimensions, some concentrating on Hofstede's four-dimensional framework (e.g. Sullivan et al., 2003), others resorting back only to the dimension of Collectivism-Individualism (e.g. Schaubroeck & Lam, 2002).

Overall research has acknowledged the importance to integrate the concepts of culture and LMX in a world in which diverse teams and cross-cultural management have become a reality (Hiller & Day, 2003). However, as the integration of the entire concepts proofs difficult to handle and is as well very complex in its results, and as concerns of validity have to be taken seriously, many researchers have opted for a more straightforward way of integrating culture and LMX. In recent studies, culture is examined as a moderator variable that acts upon the relation of LMX and its antecedents or outcomes respectively (e.g. Dulebohn et al., 2012, Rockstuhl et al., 2012; Erdogan & Liden, 2006). Depending on the focal antecedent or outcome, differing cultures are found to have differing influences on its relationship towards LMX.

This paragraph has shown that the relationships between LMX, trust and culture are widely acknowledged to be important but also complex in nature. Many researchers undertook to examine the correlations between two or three of the concepts, however for reasons of complexity a comprehensive approach integrating all three models has not yet been presented. The following section will therefore limit the concept of culture to two specific instances. By concentrating on research conducted on specific examples, more clarity can be achieved and the research questions of this study be derived.

2.5   Evidence from China and Germany

This study's interest of research concentrates on the cultural contexts of Germany and China. Both countries are directly opposed in the cultural dimensions of Individualism versus Collectivism and Power Distance. Whereas Germany is classified as being an individualist culture, reaching a score of 67 on Hofstede's scale, China is rated only 20, thus qualifying for a collectivist culture. On the other hand, China is high in Power Distance, scoring 80 on the Hofstede scale, while Germany is rated 35 only (Itim International, 2015). In accordance with the Triandis (1995) classification of culture, China can thus be categorized as a V-C culture whereas Germany represents a H-I culture. The marked cultural distance renders both countries interesting for comparison and at the same is an important base for the understanding of this paragraph. A detailed derivation of why China and Germany in particular are chosen for comparison is to be found in Chapter 3.2.

2.5.1 The Concept of Trust in China and in Germany

As was shown by the research conducted in the area of trust and culture, propensity to trust varies across societies (Fukuyama, 1995; Lane, 1998). Since scholars are discordant about whether H-I or V-C cultures display a higher general propensity to trust, every country needs to be looked at specifically (Johnson & Cullen, 2002). One means of comparing two culture's relative propensity to trust is provided by the World Values Survey (WVS), in which citizens of almost 100 different countries are questioned in regular intervals about their values and beliefs. One of the questions is phrased as follows: "Generally speaking, would you say that most people can be trusted or that you need to be very careful in dealing with people?" (WVS, 2015). Over 60% of the Chinese respondents answered that question positively, stating that they generally trust people, while only less than 45% of all Germans gave a positive reply in the 6th wave of the survey conducted between 2010 and 2014 (ibid.). It can thus be concluded that Chinese people show a larger general propensity to trust than people from Germany. This trend also holds true when members of both groups were asked about their propensity to trust different in-groups (such as their family and fellow nationals). However, it is interesting to note that the trust levels of Chinese nationals decline when asked about their propensity to trust out-group members, represented by strangers and people of different nationalities. All of a sudden the dynamic changes and Germans express greater overall trust levels towards members of perceived out-groups than Chinese do (WVS, 2015).

This finding is supported by Child and Möllering (2003), who elaborate on the absence of powerful governmental institutions in China. According to them the absence of a strong governing external factor is the underlying rationale why Chinese nationals bestow trust only on in-group members while distrusting others. While agreeing with their main finding, Johnson and Cullen (2002) take a different approach. They argue that the Chinese concept of Guanxi plays a significant role as a basis for trust. As Guanxi refers to informal ties and relationships between individuals who repeatedly exchange personal favors (Langenberg, 2007, pp. 1), Johnson and Cullen argue as well that trust is given to in-group members. However instead of stating an absence of institutions, they consider the societal order influenced by Guanxi as an informal, trust-creating institution.

Less research has been conducted on how trust is built in Germany, as from the eyes of Western researchers no such "alien" concepts as Guanxi need to be taken into account. However, Lane and Bachman (1997) noted that social institutions also play a role in trust development in Germany. Although their study primarily addresses inter-firm relationships, it still allows to draw conclusions on values preeminent in society, namely that institutional trust is derived from specific norms and standards.

When researching trust in China and in Germany, features inherent to their respective cultures need to be taken into account. Leung and Cohen (2011) point to the importance of the distinction between Dignity Cultures and Face Cultures (a concept also known as Guilt and Shame Cultures). Ayers (1984, p. 19) defines dignity as "the conviction that each individual at birth possessed an intrinsic value at least theoretically equal to that of every other person". Members of Dignity Cultures value themselves internally by their dignity that cannot be taken away by others, therefore acting independent from others. Equality is stressed and good behavior guaranteed by the internal feeling of guilt as well as the external rules of law. For this reason a person that cannot be trusted is a person who does not dispose of an inner sturdiness coming from a strong sense of dignity (Leung and Cohen, 2011). Germany as a H-I culture represents such a dignity culture.

Face on the other hand is defined as "the amount of public worth that one has associated with one's roles" (Heine, 2001, p. 899). If one cannot properly fulfill their role in society one loses face. In a Face Culture, the self is valued in its position towards others and hierarchy is emphasized. The shame resulting from losing face when behaving improperly is ensuring moral behavior. A person that is not trustworthy therefore is a person that does not show concern for the opinion of others or the threat of losing face (Leung & Cohen, 2011).

It is shown that the basis of trust formation varies between Germany and China. Different from Germany, the concept of Guanxi, form the basis of trust in China (Johnson & Cullen, 2002). Whereas in China a moral and thus trustworthy person is a person that protects their face, in Germany morality is coming from a consciousness of good and bad inside every person. Someone who is trustworthy therefore is a person that has strong convictions and acts accordingly.

2.5.2 The Concept of LMX in China and in Germany

LMX theory was originally introduced by Western researchers of H-I cultures as a concept tailored to a Western H-I cultural context. The exchange rules that guide the dyadic work relationship at the center of the construct seemed to be fast forward at the time, but proof to be multi-layered when transferred to a cross-cultural context (Cheng et al., 2015; Schyns et al., 2005).

Going back to the concept of Dignity and Face Cultures, Leung and Cohen (2011) state that rules of social exchange vary considerably between them. In a Dignity Culture relationships that are marked by fair exchange are the dominant pattern. In opposition to this, Face Cultures are marked by hierarchical social relationships in which power is distributed unequally. Not only is this finding congruent with the traits of H-I and V-C cultures, but can also be applied on the instances of China and Germany. In China, defined as V-C Face Culture, social exchanges are marked by hierarchy (Cheng et al., 2015), whereas in Germany, which qualifies as a H-I Dignity Culture, equality is stressed in an exchange relationship. As Cheng and colleagues (2015) note, different expectations in a leader or a member respectively emerge out of the differing rules of exchange. Expectations and their fulfillment in turn act directly upon the perceived LMX quality of both leader and member (Liden et al., 1993; Wayne et al., 1997; Scandura & Pelligrini, 2008).

The concept of Guanxi has been touched upon in the previous paragraph, as it constitutes an important basis for trust in China. Given that trust and LMX are strongly connected, the role of Guanxi should also not be underestimated in the context of LMX specific to China. Law and colleagues (2000) found that LMX and Guanxi are two distinct concepts, arguing that Guanxi was the "Chinese approach" to govern supervisor-subordinate relationships, while LMX was the approach specific to a Western surrounding. The main distinction between the two approaches to dyadic work relationships lies in the nature of the underlying exchange: The Western LMX approach "refers only to the supervisor-subordinate interchange within the work relationship and the benefits being exchanged are mainly work-related" (Law et al., 2000, p. 755). The Chinese concept of Guanxi on the other hand has a wider reach. Law and colleagues (2000) state that it "covers mainly non-work exchange within the vertical dyad and the benefits being exchanged can be social and economic in nature" (Law et al., 2000, p. 755). Although the researchers tie Guanxi "mainly" (ibid.) to the mutual non-work exchange, they still find that it has important implications for work-related supervisory administrative decisions such as job assignments, promotions or bonus allocations. Thus this study argues that Guanxi is broader than LMX, extending the leader-member relationship to the private sphere. As in collectivistic cultures such as China harmonious working relationships are of higher importance than in Western individualist cultures (Easterby-Smith et al., 1995), it seems natural that Guanxi is a holistic concept, covering relationships both at work and off work, thus intertwining private and business life.

Considering the hierarchical traits inherent to Chinese society in combination with the concept of Guanxi, it does not astonish that Chinese leaders traditionally take a paternalistic approach to leadership (e.g. Zhang et al., 2015). Paternalistic leadership is rooted in Confucianism and marked by strong discipline, authority with moral integrity and fatherly benevolence (Cheng et al., 2014). Chinese leaders are thus expected to behave morally, that is as a role-model of virtue, self-discipline and unselfishness, benevolent, which refers to showing interest in a subordinates personal life, his family and his well-being beyond work, and finally authoritarian, showing strength and demanding unquestionable obedience from their subordinates (Farh & Cheng, 2000). Wu and colleagues (2012) found that among the three traits of paternalistic leadership inherent to Chinese management practices, benevolence and morality are fostering trust of a subordinate in his superior, thus enhancing LMX quality, while authority has a negative effect on subordinate's trust in his supervisor, ergo also a negative effect on LMX quality.

In sharp contrast to China, Germany represents a H-I culture and thereby a member of the same cultural area in which the concept of LMX was originally coined. Exchange rules in Germany as a Dignity Culture follow the ideals of relative equality and independence from others (Leung & Cohen, 2011). Different from China, leadership in a German context is thus not marked by hierarchy, but rather by participation and autonomy (Szabo et al., 2002). Participative leadership as prevalent in Germany emphasizes the involvement of subordinates in making and impeding their supervisor's decisions (Javidan et al., 2006). LMX in a German context is thus perceived to be of high quality when a supervisor integrates his subordinate into sensitive projects and trusts him or her to successfully master challenging tasks assigned to him (Schyns et al., 2005).

High-quality LMX is tied to different expectations resulting out of differing prevalent leadership styles in China and in Germany. Whereas in China expectations of both, supervisors and subordinates arise out of the commonly applied paternalistic leadership model, they are formed by a participative leadership model in Germany. While Chinese employees expect their leader to make decisions, to lead and to care for them personally, Germans typically expect their superiors to grant them insights into their decision-making process and to trust them to autonomously tackle challenging tasks. In turn Chinese superiors expect their subordinates to act obedient and loyal towards them (Farh & Cheng, 2000), whereas German leaders expect their team-members to work independently and to voice their own thoughts (Szabo et al., 2002).

There is no debate among researchers that eastern and Western management styles differ (House et al., 2002). However, Floyd (1999) argues that along with the much referred to ongoing progress of globalization, it is becoming increasingly difficult to draw a sharp line between them. Due to an increase in international trade and Foreign Direct Investment (FDI) activities, a continued process of harmonization of standards and the ongoing integration of trading clusters such as the European Union management practices continue to merge around the globe. For similar reasons the demarcation line of national cultures is becoming blurry (e.g. Castells, 2000). This trend is likely to influence the formation of high-quality LMX in both China and Germany, moving the cultures and its leadership practices closer together, thus gradually aligning expectations of supervisors towards their subordinates and vice versa.

2.6 Research Objectives

Building on the conducted literature review in the areas of LMX, trust and culture, it becomes obvious that all three constructs have been studied intensively, yet for reasons of complexity no comprehensive approach has been pursued. Especially when focusing on LMX literature, a comprehensive model is still lacking, with the theoretical foundations of the theory being dispersed and antecedents, outcomes, dimensions as well as moderator variables on LMX not clearly defined.

Derived from the state of research, the aim of this study is twofold. On the one hand it will contribute to a more comprehensive approach towards LMX theory by qualitatively examining the influence of trust on LMX. Such an approach allows for new insights to emerge as it asks specifically for "why?" instead of solely testing dispersed hypotheses that can never yield a comprehensive picture. On the other hand, the study's intention is to extend upon LMX theory by conducting in-depth interviews with culturally diverse LM-Dyads. Such an approach can yield specific insights into the role of culture in establishing high-quality exchanges between leaders and members from two different cultural contexts. Although research has been conducted on the role of culture within LMX theory, it generally stops at looking at just one culture or highlighting differences between different cultures. So far no influential work on the emergence of high-quality LMX between partners of two different cultures has been conducted. Additionally the vast majority of conducted research took a quantitative approach (Schriesheim et al., 1999) that cannot grant comprehensive insights into underlying dynamics of building high-quality LMX.

Taking the cross-cultural LM-Dyad as unit of data collection and focus of research, this study first wants to examine whether the findings on trust and LMX yielded in a mono-cultural surrounding still hold true for a cross-cultural dyad. It will therefore inquire whether also in a cross-cultural LM-Dyad trust and LMX are connected positively. Furthermore, the study wants to take a closer look at how trust is built in the cross-cultural setting, thus expecting to derive insights on the formation of high-quality LMX relationships in a cross-cultural setting. It will be asked whether trust is valued higher by the member of one culture than by the member of the second and whether building trust in a culturally diverse LM-Dyad proves to be more difficult than in a mono-cultural LM-Dyads. Moreover it is examined whether the cross-cultural surrounding in which the LM-Dyad operates has an influence on the trust-building process. Considering the insight that expectations of both co-workers and their fulfillment directly influence perceived LMX quality (Liden et al., 1993; Wayne et al., 1997; Scandura & Pelligrini, 2008) as well as the level of trust bestowed on the co-worker (Colquitt et al., 2007), it is inquired in how far the different expectations in leadership that the co-workers bring into the relationship play a role in the trust-building and LMX developing process. Finally, building upon Floyd's (1999) as well as House and colleagues' (2002) insights that cultures continue to merge, it is asked whether detected differences are a phenomenon that is markedly decreasing with age.

By addressing these research questions, the study wants to contribute to LMX literature in providing comprehensive answers. Furthermore it aims at expanding the field of research to cross-cultural LM-Dyads.

3   Methodology

In order to answer the research questions derived in Chapter 2.6, a qualitative study has been conducted, in the course of which leaders and members of nine culturally diverse LM-Dyads were interviewed. All of the interviewees were employed either in the Chinese subsidiary or Joint Venture of a German MNC operating in Mainland China. The following section describes the applied research methodology by first discussing the research design and research setting. Subsequently the method and process of data collection is highlighted. The chapter closes by outlining the applied scheme of data analysis.

3.1   Research Design

Rockstuhl and colleagues (2012) reported close to 600 studies that have been dealing with LMX theory since its conceptualization in 1975. However, scholars repeatedly criticized the absence of a consolidated theory (e.g. Schriesheim et al., 1999; Cropanzano & Mitchell, 2005), while also stating that "the major theoretical papers number only a few" (Schriesheim et al., 1999, p. 100). The vast majority of research has been conducted following a quantitative approach, thus examining antecedents and outcomes of LMX as well as various moderating variables (Dulebohn et al., 2012). While this approach allows for deductive testing of diverse hypotheses, thus revealing connections between different variables (Stokes & Wall, 2014, p. 98), researchers have not been able to inductively theorize and further consolidate LMX theory (Schriesheim et al., 1999). Only qualitative research can address the structural problems reported throughout LMX research by in-depth inquiries, revealing connections that cannot be seen using quantitative methods and adding factors to the broader picture that cannot be found solely deductively (Rubin & Rubin, 2012, p. xv; Bryman & Bell, 2011, pp. 26ff.).

As this study is intending to understand the various and multi-leveled influences trust has on LMX in LM-Dyads composed of co-workers with different nationalities, the research aim is considered too complex to be sufficiently addressed by quantitative research (Birkinshaw et al., 2011). A qualitative approach can answer Schriesheim and colleagues' call for more comprehensive research. In addition it allows for an in-depth inquiry of the underlying rationales of the trust-building process and how they influence the leader-member exchange. Especially as LMX is in itself a dyadic approach, it seems rational as well as necessary to focus research attention directly on the exchange processes between leaders and members of working dyads (Anand et al., 2011). Unlike many prior studies, data for this work has thus been extracted from in-depth interviews with both partners of LM-Dyads. Although the research design aims at validating existent research by deductive inquiries in an attempt to contribute to the answer of Schriesheim and colleague's call for consolidation of LMX theory, the applied method of semi-structured interviews also gives way for inductive theory building (Eriksson & Kovalainen, 2008, p. 82). Therefore the research design allows new, to date unobserved factors to emerge and to be added to the existent body of research.

First and foremost the study is an explanatory one, aiming to understand the underlying rationales of the trust-building process between co-workers of different cultures and their implications for LMX theory (Saunders et al., 2012, p. 172). However, as to date not many studies investigated upon cross-cultural LM-Dyads, it is considered important that the research design also allows for the option of inductive theory building in order not to repeat the negligence of prior research.

3.2   Research Setting

Scandura and Lankau (1996) note that although the concept of LMX has already been thoroughly investigated, little attention has been directed to the issue of diversity, in particular the issue of cultural diversity. While in subsequent years authors have addressed the identified research gap (e.g. Duncan & Herrera, 2014), no recognized studies focusing on the culturally diverse LM-Dyad as unit of data collection can be detected. Answering Scandura and Lankau's call for a closer examination of the connection of LMX theory and diversity research, all of the nine interviewed LM-Dyads of this study are composed of culturally diverse co-workers. In each case one employee is of German nationality, whereas his or her partner stems from Mainland China. In one special case the German co-worker is of Turkish origin, but as he attended German schools early on, lived and worked in Germany for the largest part of his life and gathered management experience exclusively in a German working environment, the matter of origin only plays a minor role in this case and can be neglected for the purpose of this study.

The two countries were chosen for various reasons. First, for a long time US-American and Japanese management practices dominated cross-cultural management theory, whereas the German approach has been "disproportionately underrepresented in the English-language management literature" (Holden, 2008, p. 9). However, Pudelko (2006) argues that German management systems are of equal importance to those of the USA and Japan, as the country is the leading economy of Europe and as such represents one of the three worldwide leading economies of the triad of North America, Europe and Asia (Eurostat, 2015). Thus the study aims at contributing to the often unrecognized body of German management literature.

Second, with an average GDP growth rate of 10% annually during the last two decades, the economy of the People's Republic of China has emerged to become the world's largest economy in terms of GDP based on purchasing power parity (PPP) in 2014 (IMF, 2015). Additionally it is the world's largest recipient of FDI (OECD, 2014) as well as the globally largest consumer market, representing almost 20% of the world's population (World Population Statistics, 2014). The sheer weight of China's economy and it's growing importance in the globally integrated world economy make the country an influential factor that cannot be ignored in management literature. Dealing with Chinese management practices has thus become a necessity for relevant modern-day business research. Hout and Michael go as far as to predict the future of management techniques in the middle of the Western and the Chinese approach, with both sides having "much to learn from each other" (2014, p. 107).

Moreover, with China being Germany's third largest trading partner and largest trading partner outside the European Union (Federal Statistical Office, 2014) while Germany being China's fourth largest trading partner worldwide and largest European trading partner (National Bureau of Statistics of China, 2014) both countries are linked by close economic ties. This factor highlights the importance of the respective partner's business conduct. When considering that the People's Republic of China (PRC) is furthermore Germany's largest recipient of FDI outside the European Union (OECD, 2014), it becomes clear that the matter of cross-cultural exchange and leadership is of current importance to both countries. By focusing exclusively on German-Chinese LM-Dyads the study can contribute to current managerial issues in both countries, adding to a better understanding of their respective partner's leadership practices and how to cope with them.

One can argue that the issue of diversity could be better addressed by focusing not only on two differing cultures, but by including members of more cultures into the sample. However, following Hofstede's (1980) groundbreaking approach to cultural dimensionality it becomes clear that Germany and China are directly opposed in the dimensions of individualism (China = 20, Germany = 67), Power Distance (China = 80, Germany = 35) and Uncertainty Avoidance (China = 30, Germany = 65) (Itim International, 2015). Accounting for the cultural values Hofstede's studies attributes to China and Germany respectively and connecting them with Triandis' (1995) framework of culture, China can be classified as a V-C Culture, whereas Germany represents a H-I Culture. Furthermore, when going back to the model of high- and low-context cultures as introduced by Hall (1976), Germany can be classified as low-context culture whereas China represents a high-context culture. Focusing thus solely on members of the two, directly opposed cultures is considered to be yielding more specific results and can thus contribute more precisely to the issue of cultural diversity in LMX theory, especially since the sample size is comparatively small.

The final rationales for focusing on members of Chinese and German culture are origin and education of the interviewer and author of the study. As she is a native German, she speaks the mother tongue of half of the interviewees, which not only facilitated a good rapport with the interviewees (Tenzer et al., 2014), but also helped her to better interpret the cultural background of the respondents and to make sense of their accounts (Morgan & Smircich, 1980). Furthermore, the interviewer has gathered expertise in the Chinese culture by living in the PRC for a total of two years, thereby learning the language and being able to communicate fluently in everyday live. The experience similarly yielded understanding for the second culture under research that goes beyond mere observation.

At the time of the investigation, all respondents were employed in either a Chinese subsidiary of a German MNC or Chinese-German Joint Venture located in Mainland China. Chang and Taylor (1999, p. 542) remark that MNCs are "essentially [...] workplaces where different ethnicities and cultural values are intertwined". Thus, it can be argued in line with Roth and Kostova (2003, p. 888) that for reasons of diversity and complexity the MNC represents a particularly suitable research context for the purpose of "validation and expansion of existent theories", in this case for a contribution to the consolidation and the expansion of the body of LMX research. The fact that the organizations of all participants in the study are located in Mainland China underlines the focus on the particular cultural diversity of China and Germany. More importantly, it aims at consistency and comparability of the findings. Subsidiaries of German MNEs operating in Hong Kong, Macau or Taiwan were explicitly excluded from the study, given the differing historical and political background that influences culture and working environment (e.g. So, 2011; Shaw, 2009).

However, within the boundaries of defined cultures, diversity among the interviewees was obtained in terms of gender, age, leader/member nationality, tenure of the dyad and experience in the respective foreign culture. This setting should allow for a broad content base of interview data to emerge (Tenzer et al., 2014), thus making way to inductively derive contributions to LMX theory as well as to deductively adding to the consolidation of the body of research (Mantere & Ketokivi, 2013).

When screening potential interview partners, it was paid attention that the tenure of the LM-Dyad had lasted at least half a year in order to guarantee both co-workers had have enough time to adapt to their counterpart's management style. The so-called "role finding" phase (Graen & Uhl-Bien, 1991, p. 32), which is the relatively short initial period of reciprocal acquaintance, in which both partners get to know each other and learn about the counterpart's abilities and characteristics (ibid.) should have been overcome. It was also considered that research has identified a positive albeit small correlation between trust and relationship duration (Vanneste et al., 2014), why tenures below 6 months were considered too short to yield profound insights. However, by interviewing partners with differing lengths of LM-Dyad tenure different stages in the relationship building process and thus also different stages in the LMX development process (Graen & Uhl-Bien, 1991) could be investigated. An overview of the defining characteristics of the interrogated LM-Dyads is provided in Figure 5.

Dyad	Role	Nationality	Gender	Age	Tenure of Cooperation	Nature of Relationship	Prior Experience with Partner's Culture	Duration of Recorded Interviews	No. of Transcript Pages
A	A-L	German	♂	56	4 Years	Senior Management	none	1:10:28	18
	A-M	Chinese	♂	48		Mid Level Management, Direct Report	none	1:11:03	16
								2:21:31	**34**
B	B-L	German	♂	44	3 Years	Managing Director	positive	0:53:57	19
	B-M	Chinese	♀	30		Assistant	none	0:34:58	13
								1:28:55	**32**
C	C-L	German	♂	56	2 Years	Mid Level Management	positive	0:31:04	10
	C-M	Chinese	♂	32		Assigned Employee, Direct Report	extensive	0:46:13	15
								1:17:17	**25**
D	D-L	German	♀	34	1 Year	Mid Level Management	marginal	0:48:34	15
	D-M	Chinese	♂	30		Assigned Employee, Direct Report	positive	0:46:46	19
								1:35:20	**34**
E	E-L	German	♂	43	1.5 Years	Senior Management	marginal	0:52:38	17
	E-M	Chinese	♀	35		Mid Level Management, Direct Report	extensive	1:05:08	20
								1:57:46	**37**
F	F-L	German	♂	45	0.5 Years	Mid Level Management	positive	0:41:53	15
	F-M	Chinese	♀	29		Assistant	positive	0:58:00	17
								1:39:53	**32**
G	G-L	Chinese	♂	41	0.5 Years	Mid Level Management	positive	0:56:34	19
	G-M	German	♂	43		Assigned Employee, Direct Report	extensive	0:54:36	26
								1:51:10	**45**
H	H-L	German	♂	47	4 Years	Mid Level Management	none	0:43:53	14
	H-M	Chinese	♀	43		Assigned Employee, Direct Report	positive	0:46:26	15
								1:30:19	**29**
I	I-L	German	♂	43	1.2 Years	Senior Management	none	0:18:17	6
	I-M	Chinese	♂	42		Mid Level Management, Direct Report	positive	0:39:52	18
								0:58:09	**24**
								14:40:20	**292**

L = Leader
M = Member

None: No prior exposure to the other culture
Marginal: Occasional exposure to the other culture, including short business trips or private travels
Positive: Exposure to the other culture, including living abroad for a short period or regular contact to members of the other culture
Extensive: Strong exposure to the other culture, including living abroad for more than half a year

Figure 5: Overview of Investigated LM-Dyads

3.3 Data Collection

The collected set of data consists of 18 semi-structured interviews, conducted in 2015 throughout different cities in Mainland China. As the qualitative research method of interviewing gives us "access to the observations of others" (Weiss, 1994, p. 1) and allows for the gathering of "rich data from people in various roles and situations" (Myers, 2008, p. 119) it is a particularly useful instrument to address the research questions about the influence of trust on LMX in a culturally diverse setting. The semi-structured approach was chosen in line with the aim of the study, which is to contribute to the consolidation as well as to the extension of LMX literature. While pre-formulated questions guarantee a certain degree of consistency across the interviews and allow for inquiries of concrete instances, the free arrangement and formulation of questions also allows for unexpected factors to emerge during the conversation (Myers, 2008, p. 122). In a semi-structured approach the interviewer is guided by the questions, but can deviate from the formulation or the topic in order to pursue an emergent train of thought (Eriksson & Kovalainen, 2008, p. 82). He is thus able to detect a priori unthought-of connections or determining factors while at the same time being able to check for recurrent patterns and robustness of prior research. The interviews were conducted following a problem-centered approach, thus building the pre-formulated questions on the findings of prior research and using them to guide interviewees to the core arguments of interest (Witzel, 2000).

The interview outline consisted of six broad topic areas whereas each conversation started out with a brief introduction part in which interviewees were asked to provide background information. This entailed demographic information about themselves and their working experience as well as rough parameters on their foreign experience and relationship towards their co-worker. The subsequent three topic areas further followed the problem-centered approach (Witzel, 2000) by gradually advancing to the core of the research questions. In order to unravel interviewees' perception about how trust influences their working relationship towards their co-worker they were first asked about the initial expectations they brought into the relationship. As prior findings point out, expectations in leaders and members vary across cultures (e.g. Cheng et al., 2015; Leung & Cohen, 2011) and act directly upon perceived LMX quality (Liden et al., 1993; Wayne et al., 1997; Scandura & Pelligrini, 2008). Furthermore they may influence perceived trustworthiness, which is why the topic area aims at a priori identifying potentially differing measures of high-quality LMX and trustworthiness. Building on the expectations towards their co-worker, participants were thus asked about how they perceive the quality of the working relationship with their partner. This section aims at determining whether the quality of Leader Member Exchange can be classified as high-quality LMX or rather low-quality LMX (Dansereau et al., 1975). Finally and switching from the general to the concrete case, interviewees are questioned about the perceived trustworthiness of their counterpart, thus reaching the core of the research question that allows to examine the connection between trust and LMX in culturally diverse LM-Dyads. Following on the sections that lead towards an answer of the research questions of this study, participants were questioned about two additional topics, trust and fairness, which will not be included to the assessment of the interviews. Although the topic areas were arranged in a spiral logic leading gradually deeper towards the answer of the research question, the order of the topics remained flexible during the interviews in order to follow the interviewees' individual train of thoughts, thus ensuring in-depth inquiries of the topics (Eriksson & Kovalainen, 2008, p. 82). The interview outline is to be found in the Appendix.

Interviews with German participants were conducted exclusively in German language, as it is the native tongue of both interviewees and interviewer. A common language increases interpersonal trust (e.g. Tenzer et al., 2014; Neely, 2013) and is therefore a valuable tool to encourage rich accounts of the respondents' experiences (Rubin & Rubin, 2012, p. 108). In spite of this conviction, interviews with Chinese employees were conducted almost exclusively in English, which is all participants' business language. As the areas of interest entail very specific vocabulary, they go beyond everyday life terminology and a superior language proficiency is needed in order to extract meaning out of the responses. Considering the given parameters of language skills of both interviewer and interviewees, the risk of loosing meaning in the process of translation (Rubin & Rubin, 2012, pp. 185) was considered smaller when conducting the interviews in English instead of Chinese language.

With the participants' permission, all interviews were recorded to facilitate a detailed analysis of the interviewees' accounts. Recording allows to recall specific details during the phase of data analysis and to analytically interpret respondents' statements (Dresing & Pehl, 2012, p. 20). A total length of 14 hours and 40 minutes of interviews was collected.

3.4 Data Analysis

Already during the process of data collection, interviews were transcribed in accordance with the "simple transcription rules" (Dresing & Pehl, 2012, p. 22) based on the work of Kuckartz and colleagues (2008, p. 27). It is argued that the simple rules - as opposed to the "complex rules" (Dresing & Pehl, 2012, p. 22) - suffice the cause of focusing on the semantic content of the interviews (ibid.). Among the most distinguished features of the simple transcription rules is the literal transcription of every word while correcting the language for dialects, slang and filler words. Non-verbal expressions of the speakers, such as laughter are reported in brackets; incomprehensible statements are marked with (incomprehensible). Each speaker is transcribed in separate paragraphs, respectively ending with a time marker in order to be able to connect the statements of each interviewee with the record, thus guaranteeing traceability and scientific accuracy. After transcripts are completed, coding the names of the interviewees anonymizes them. Anonymization is achieved by numbering each LM-Dyad alphabetically. Leaders are then marked with "L", their members on a subordinate hierarchical level with "M". For example the leader of the third interviewed LM-Dyad will thus be marked with C-L and the member of the fifth interrogated LM-Dyad with E-M. This coding system allows for scientific accuracy and traceability while at the same time protecting the interviewees' identity. Moreover, company names as well as city names that allow for inference on the interviewee's company were substituted with [Company Name] or [City Name] in order to protect company internal information that may be considered sensitive[2].

---

2   The published version of the study additionally abstains from marking direct quotes with the described abbreviations in order to respect the anonymity of the respondents.

All transcripts have been written down literally in the language the interview was conducted in. German statements that are quoted throughout the study are translated into English and marked with [tr]. In sum a total amount of 292 single-spaced pages was extracted from the conducted interviews.

As Auerbach and Silverstein (2003, p. 31) define, "theory, is a description of a pattern that you find in the data". Therefore, in order to answer the research questions and to build theory with the obtained set of raw data, patterns needed to be traced within the transcripts. As the amount of extracted data is too massive and too complex to discover repetitive answers between the interviewees on first glance, transcripts were coded with the qualitative research software Atlas.ti, following the advice of Kuckartz and colleagues (2008, p. 36). During the process, every passage of the interviews is read and phrases, sentences or also paragraphs that seem to convey thoughts connected to the research question are marked and assigned a code, that is either a word or a phrase that summarizes the idea of the text segment. For example one interviewee said that in China the corporate culture resembled a "boss culture". Thus the code "boss culture" was introduced and assigned to subsequent quotes that similarly referred to the importance of hierarchical leadership in China. In other instances, codes were assigned that did not emerge out of the speaker's phrasing, but were rather related to concepts known in literature or interpreted by the interviewer and assigned a certain context. For example one interviewee reflected: "What we take for right in our world is either not important here or it comes in another shape" [tr]. The statement was interpreted as reflecting the well-known concept of the "Cultural Gap" and thus coded correspondingly.

After all interviews were processed accordingly, codes were reviewed and checked for interferences. Consequently, codes were merged in order to better circumvent separate ideas. Subsequently codes were clustered into certain categories, such as "Expectations", "LMX" or "Trust-building" (Auerbach & Silverstein, 2003, p. 36). Throughout each category, opinions of the group of Chinese employees were juxtaposed to the quotations of the group of German employees, as well as the ideas of the leaders were contrasted with the statements of the members. Furthermore, the interviews of each LM-Dyad were juxtaposed in order to gain insights in the reciprocity of their exchange. By comparing the codes between groups, patterns became obvious and connections between codes were detected.

Prior to the collection of the primary data as described above, a secondary literature review was conducted. Searching the electronic databases EBSCO, JSTOR and Google Scholar, seminal writings in the area of LMX, trust, and diversity research were traced (Stokes & Wall, 2014, p. 47), along with the historical evolution of theory in the respective areas (ibid., p. 49). Central debates and disagreements were subsumed. By comparing the insights gained from the secondary literature review to the emergent patterns in the primary data, propositions could be extracted and findings tied to existent research.

4 Findings and Propositions

The following section will present the main findings of the conducted study and tie them to previous scholars' work. By addressing the research questions outlined in Chapter 2.6 theoretical propositions are derived. The section is structured along thematic blocs that could be derived from the extracted data. First, the importance of trust for both supervisors and subordinates across cultures will be examined. Subsequently focus is laid on the element of culture and how it influences the development of both trust and LMX. Finally, the process of cultural approximation is investigated and conclusions on its relevance for trust formation and LMX development in cross-cultural LM-Dyads are drawn.

4.1 The Importance of Trust in Cross-Cultural LM-Dyads

As outlined in paragraph 2.4.1, researchers agree that trust and high-quality LMX are strongly interrelated, with some scholars going as far as to name trust a "necessary precondition for entering into and developing a high-quality dyadic relationship" (Sue-Chan et al., 2012, p. 459). However, as the finding has been derived from a mono-cultural context only, this study aims at investigating whether it still holds true in a cross-cultural context. By inquiring whether trust and LMX are positively connected in a culturally diverse LM-Dyad, the first research question is thus addressed in the introductory bloc of findings. Moreover, it is found that previous studies derived their insights mainly from quantitative studies (Schriesheim et al., 1999). The qualitative approach of this work yields the possibility to draw conclusions on the underlying rationales that connect trust and LMX (Bryman & Bell, 2011, p. 27). It is thus asked how trust is built in a cross-cultural work relationship and whether, irrespectively of the component of culture, it yields high-quality LMX for both members of cross-cultural LM-Dyads. Building on the emergent findings the third research question is addressed, inquiring whether members of differing cultures value trust differently.

In addressing the first research question, all 18 interviewees were asked about whether they consider trust to be an important factor in their working relationship. Responses were unambiguously positive, with all of the interviewees agreeing that trust is the foundation of an effective working relationship. One interviewee states blunt and clear:

"Without trust we could not work!"

When further asked why trust has a positive influence on their working relationship, interviewees agree that it facilitates positive work outcomes. Another participant of the study simply but accordingly replies:

"I think trust makes things easier."

Although especially leaders seem to be aware that trust can also be abused, they still consider it necessary to establish trustful, functioning working relationships with their subordinates. When asked whether he considers trust to play an important role in the working relationship towards his subordinate, a German leader comments:

"Maybe limiting trust at certain points plays a role just as important." [tr]

However, he further elaborates on his statement, saying:

"It [i.e. trust] shouldn't be a blind one, [...] but especially in a long-lasting relationship and when you work together closely, you have to say for certain topics that he or she is in charge, she's doing it and I take it as it is." [tr]

Although as a leader he isn't willing to distribute trust easily, he is still convinced that without trust entirely an efficient working relationship would not exist.

Some interviewees go even further, hinting that in a cross-cultural context trust may be of even greater importance than when dealing with members of the same cultural background. The following statement of a Chinese manager is exemplary for cross-cultural problems that can be overcome by the development of trust:

"I think, because of the different culture, and all people, sometimes the German side and the Chinese side maybe feels 'oh we can't fully understand your idea, I can't accept your idea'. Trust is maybe related to accepting these things. Accept."

In its essence, this quote reveals how the differing cultural background of leader and member first fosters a certain degree of distrust, that is "the opposite of trust" (Lewicki et al., 1998, p. 439). In their theory-generating approach, Tenzer and colleagues (2014) found, that especially differing language is an element that hinders the formation of trust in multinational teams (MNT). Due to a lack of cultural as well as linguistic understanding, opinions and behavior of the foreign co-worker are hard to grasp and because they are not understood intuitively they give cause to suspicion. Therefore, bestowing trust on a team member in a cross-cultural context means that suspicion can be overcome and thus way is made for effective working relationships and the formation of high-quality LMX relationships.

It is found, that all interviewees agree on the general importance of trust in a working relationship. Trust seems to be even more important in a cross-cultural LM-Dyad as it can help to overcome cultural ambiguities and thus substitutes for a lack of cultural knowledge or language skills. As a basis for further findings it is therefore proposed that:

Proposition 1a: Trust has a positive influence on LMX, especially in culturally diverse LM-Dyads.

Trust researchers have found, that although both trust and LMX contain reciprocity, they do not necessarily need to be balanced (Brower et al., 2000). Literature has mostly examined trust from the perspective of the subordinate (Dirks & Ferrin, 2001), assuming that positive outcomes of trust in a working relationship are mainly derived from the subordinate's trust in his supervisor. Only in 2009 Brower and colleagues laid focus on the reciprocal trust exchanged between leaders and members, finding that a supervisor's trust in his or her subordinate yields equally positive outcomes on the subordinate's performance at the workplace. A mutually trusting relationship can thus foster high-quality LMX for both members of the LM-Dyad. However, Brower and colleagues' study followed a quantitative approach, measuring responses from LM-Dyads in a Western environment. As this study aims at verifying their findings for a cross-cultural context, it is examined whether trust plays an important role for both, leaders and members of differing cultural background.

When asked whether the relationship to the subordinate has become better over time, a German leader states:

> *"Yes, of course, because I can give many things into his care and don't need to check on them anymore. That's why meanwhile there are many things I can say I blindly trust he will take care of them. And I don't double check because I know I left it in good hands." [tr]*

In accordance with Rousseau and colleagues (1998) as well as Miles and Creed (1995), this statement exemplifies that trust is built up over time and consequently leads to a gradual improvement of LMX. From the supervisor's perspective, the relationship is rendered more efficient as tasks can be delegated to the subordinate. The established trust allows to leave them entirely in his hands without investing additional time to double check the delegated duties.

Although the trust he bestows on his superior has to be different in nature, the respective subordinate agrees:

> *"And then you can trust each other little, little. And finally of course for the business, maybe you can tell him or her what is my problem. And also you can ask him or her 'Can you help me?' or 'What can you do for me?' And then he will think about what I can do for you. And then also fast you can get some benefit."*

The gradual improvement of trust yields high-quality LMX for the subordinate as well. However, in his perspective trust has a positive impact on the exchange with his leader as it first and foremost allows him to approach his superior with questions or the request for support.

Although the underlying rationales of why trust yields high-quality LMX are different for superiors and subordinates, both parties coincide about its importance. Considering furthermore that participants of this study unambiguously agree that trust forms the basis for an effective working relationship, it can be concluded that trust plays an important role for both Germans and Chinese in gradually developing high-quality LMX. As the LM-Dyad consistent of a Chinese superior and a German subordinate likewise agree that trust forms the basis of their exchange, the finding is verified for the roles of both, leaders and members. As a second basic proposition it is therefore concluded that:

Proposition 1b: Trust yields high-quality LMX for both co-workers in a culturally diverse LM-Dyad.

It is one of the main interests of this study to examine potential differences in the way trust influences LMX in China as opposed to Germany. Theory hereby implicates that trust is built up differently in China as compared to Germany. It was found in Chapter 2.5 that the concept of Guanxi is omnipresent in Chinese V-C society, guiding the rules of social exchange and representing a social institution that possesses the potential to create trust (Johnson & Cullen, 2002). It is therefore examined whether the concept influences the establishment of high-quality LMX in China.

Guanxi is defined as informal ties and relationships between individuals who repeatedly exchange personal favors (Langenberg, 2007, pp. 1). In order to measure the concept, Farh and colleagues (1998) proposed eight particularistic ties that indicate the presence of Guanxi: Whether former classmates, relatives, individuals with the same last name, the same natal origin, former colleagues, former teachers or students, former bosses or subordinates and former neighbors, all connections imply the presence of a "shared social experience" (Farh et al., 1998, p. 473) that establishes the ties known as Guanxi in China. Chinese participants of this study accordingly confirmed that a personal connection based on Guanxi yields trust.

> *"It's my personal habit, that before I meet a new person, a stranger [...], firstly I will tell myself it's a good person. I should, and I am capable to hold good communication with the coming person. And maybe it's from my company, it's from my friends, it's from my school... This way I always know they're not bad people."*

While Guanxi yields trust, LMX is based on trust as was shown in the previous paragraph. In order to unravel the influence trust and Guanxi have on LMX, interviewees were questioned whether they think that the word "relationship" in the term "work relationship" had a stronger importance in China than in Germany. A Chinese subordinate gives an important insight:

"For the personal relationship, I think in China it's more important. It's more important than the working relationship. [...] If the personal relationship is very good then you can do something very easily, even if you don't have experience in this area, you can also easily deal with something."

This statement illustrates how Guanxi can open doors in China that are closed without personal connections. Law and colleagues (2000) find, that Guanxi between a supervisor and a subordinate in traditional Chinese LM-Dyads can be potent to the point that they influence the supervisor's administrative decisions such as bonus allocations or promotions, even if the benefits are not objectively earned by the qualification of the recipient. A Chinese interviewee confirms:

"Before there's many, you know, national company, and in the old national company, relationship is more important than ability. You must have really good relationship with your boss, then you can have the, you know, possibility to get a promotion."

Based on this statement it is justified to ask whether the concept of Guanxi is valued higher in traditional China than the concept of LMX. However, it has to be kept in mind, that the ultimate purpose of establishing trust and thereby high-quality LMX in a Western context is to achieve favorable work outcomes for both, supervisor and subordinate (Dienesch & Liden, 1986). Although LMX and Guanxi are found to be distinct concepts (Law et al., 2000), they both ultimately serve the same purpose: Positive work outcomes for superiors and subordinates.

In traditional China however, these goals are not mainly achieved by iteratively building trustful, high-quality LMX between subordinate and supervisor, but through a relationship that is marked by reciprocal and repeated exchange of personal favors. A Chinese interviewee with a profound understanding for the Chinese tradition commented:

"I think the German experts and the German colleagues like [that] the business is the business, the connection is the connection. They subject the things [...]. They only do the business, don't consider any connection, relationship and the people feeling. They only focus on the business. They only focus on the, talk the business. The Chinese usually, because you know the Chinese have the 5.000 years of history. And usually from the old roads the

parents they like the traditional philosophy. They usually, the business have some relationship and the connections."

Different from Germany, Guanxi, that is the cited relationship and the connections, plays an important role in the achievement of work related goals in a Chinese cultural context. As found in Chapter 2.5, Guanxi hereby is a broader concept than LMX, including the co-workers' personal lives (Law et al., 2000), whereas LMX predominant in Western contexts is limited to the working sphere. The statement quoted above clearly reveals that the limitation of the business relationship to the working sphere is hard to grasp in traditional Chinese understanding.

In the Chinese approach, trust is a result that emerges out of Guanxi and is deeply intertwined with it. While Guanxi is based mainly on institution-based trust in the beginning (Johnson & Cullen, 2002), LMX is enhanced mostly by CBT (Scandura & Pelligrini, 2008) in its initial stages. IBT becomes important for both Guanxi and LMX over time (Scandura & Pelligrini, 2008; Rousseau et al., 1998; Johnson & Cullen, 2002).

Although the trust emergent from Guanxi is contributing to a high-quality LMX, it similarly allows for taking a "short-cut" by directly yielding positive work related outcomes. In traditional China Guanxi alone is sufficient to yield favorable work outcomes, whereas in a Western context such an option is non-existent and would instead be paralleled with nepotism or bribery (Li, 2013). The following figure depicts the relationships of trust, LMX and Guanxi in China and Germany respectively, as derived from this study's findings.

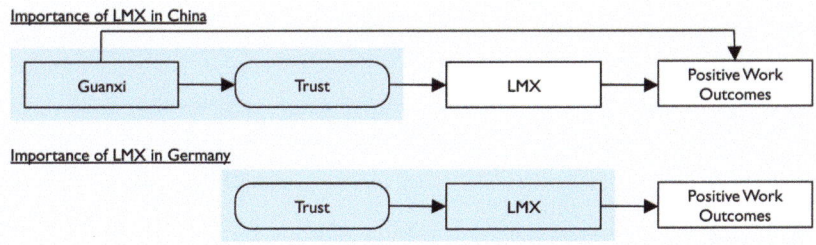

Figure 6: Importance of LMX in China and in Germany

Based on the finding that Guanxi is more important in yielding favorable work outcomes in traditional China than in Germany, it is proposed that:

Proposition 1c: In the German cultural context trust is more important for the development of a positive working relationship than in the Chinese cultural context, where more emphasis is laid on the concept of Guanxi.

It is found in this paragraph that trust is the foundation of a successful und efficient working relationship in cross-cultural LM-Dyads. Without trust collaboration is rendered difficult and inefficient. Whereas trust is important in both cultural contexts, it is found that in China another element needs to be taken into account. The concept of Guanxi, rooted deep in Chinese culture, is an important trust generator based on a person's social identity and allows to shorten the generally lengthy process of iterative trust formation. In a traditional Chinese background Guanxi can trump trust and proofs to be a more powerful tool in achieving desirable work outcomes.

4.2 The Influence of Culture on Trust and LMX

It was pointed out in Chapter 2.5 that leadership styles predominant in the German and in the Chinese business context vary due to cultural differences. Whereas in China traditionally a paternalistic approach to leadership is pursued (Zhang et al., 2015), a participative approach is favored in Germany (Szabo et al., 2002). As members of each culture are educated in the respectively applied approach to leadership, they consequently bring differing expectations in supervisors and subordinates to a cross-cultural LM-Dyad. Since expectations of both co-workers are found to influence trust formation as well as LMX quality (Colquitt et al., 2007; Scandura & Pelligrini, 2008), it is the aim of this study to identify and contrast potentially differing requirements of Chinese and German supervisors and subordinates. Doing so can help to avoid cultural clashes within cross-cultural LM-Dyads and thus contribute to developing an efficient working relationship marked by high-quality LMX. The second thematic bloc of findings therefore addresses the research questions connected to the formation of trust.

It is examining whether trust and LMX are built up differently across cultures, whether consequently the establishment of high-quality LMX proves to be more difficult in a cross-cultural LM-Dyad than in a mono-cultural LM-Dyad and finally, whether the cultural setting provided by MNEs influences the trust-building process with an impact on LMX.

When Chinese participants of this study were asked about the general expectations they have in a supervisor, a pattern emerged after evaluating only a few answers. As derived from the interviewees' responses, the ideal leader in a Chinese context is a person who is assertive, who supports his subordinates and ideally is omniscient so that he can act as a role model and teacher. A Chinese subordinate who functions as supervisor towards his own team as well describes exemplarily:

> *"My experience of one supervisor, he is really strong. [...] He gives a lot of tough discussions, even really fighting. I have to say it's really fighting discussion between departments. So I know some guys will really like this kind of manager because they really feel the support from the back side."*

German supervisors in turn have a different understanding of how to fulfill their role as a leader. Based on the prevalent participative leadership style in Germany they expect their subordinates to work independently and to voice their own thoughts in discussions (Szabo et al., 2002). The differing interpretation of a leader's responsibility often leads to cultural clashes on both the Chinese and the German side. A Chinese subordinate who spent time in Germany comments insightfully:

> *"Chinese [...] expect their boss to be like a superman or superwoman. That means they are a role model, they know always better than themselves. This is a very different expectation from a Chinese employee to a German employee. And I also remember that when my supervisor, when my boss said 'I don't know. You should know better than me!' I was very shocked!"*

On the other hand, German supervisors in China often feel overwhelmed by the Chinese expectation to be omniscient. A German leader explains:

> *"It's getting annoying when they consult me for every minor task. When they come with a tool sketch and it depicts an edge of 45° times 0.5 and they ask: 'Can it also be 0.7?' I just answer: 'Am I God?' " [tr]*

When Germans in contrast were asked about their general expectations in a subordinate the answer "quality of the delivered work" ranked first. This finding coincides with Brodbeck and colleague's (2002) study about German leadership, in which they find that performance orientation as the most pronounced German cultural value is reflected in the German leadership style. A German supervisor exemplarily summarizes his expectations in a subordinate:

> " [...] that he is flexible, able to work under pressure, that he fulfills his assigned tasks without several check-ups, in short that he works precisely and has fun in his job." [tr]

However, interviewees stated regularly that their expectations conflicted with the Chinese understanding of delegation. Whereas in a German context it is important to work independently, Chinese are used to superiors determining their schedule and guiding them closely. Germans however show little understanding for thoughtless and thus perceived as carelessly conducted work. A German supervisor complains:

> "There are also things where I'd say, one could have maybe thought a little bit about it, that you could avoid them. I mean like logical fractures somewhere in a presentation or jumping to a conclusion that, maybe if you take two or three minutes... and most of the times, or I'd say my critique on the working style, is trying to finish something as fast as possible to be able to switch to the next task. The job in itself is not really important it is much more about getting it done quickly." [tr]

Others agree with him, that emphasis of Chinese subordinates is placed more on quantity than on quality.

> "We're positioned very differently in Europe. For us, when we see we can't finish something on time we possess the greatness and the courage to go to our boss and to say 'I did this and that, I won't be able to finish that in time, give me two more months.' But here a culture of punishment exists when you are not done in time [...] and that scares off the workers from openly admitting that they cannot deliver something perfectly. In many cases I discovered that leaders are not able and therefore also don't double check whether they got a perfect result. For them, too, it is important to report to

their superiors that an attempt was made. Everything done. But what was the result of the attempt again?" [tr]

Just as Germans often feel overwhelmed by Chinese expectations, it is also difficult from a Chinese point of view to understand the German expectations and act accordingly.

"For example sometimes I guess I do some PPT, presentations. And probably sometimes it has not fulfilled the quality, it has not fulfilled his expectations. And then later I will give some more, more do this work."

This statement of a Chinese subordinate is exemplary for the difficulties posed by a foreign superior with different expectations. Earlier in this paragraph it was pointed out that the differing expectations both leaders and members bring to a working relationship will finally influence the development of trust and determine the quality of the exchange (Colquitt et al., 2007; Scandura & Pelligrini, 2008). When asked why they can trust their co-worker, Chinese as well as Germans replied accordingly that their partners had fulfilled the expectations they had in them. A German leader thus states:

"Why I trust someone... Well, trust is built up by actions according to my expectations I think. That means in how far are my expectations fulfilled, including unexpressed ones." [tr]

When asked why he perceives his German subordinate as trustworthy, a Chinese supervisor accordingly replies:

"I have to say he understands what I expected."

Building on the different expectations of both Chinese and Germans in their respective supervisors/subordinates in conjunction with the finding that trust is build up by "actions according to expectations" it can be concluded that trust is built up by differing criteria across cultures.

However, the majority of interviewees agrees that with regard to their partner's expectations a learning process occurred. Finally the achieved improvements translated into a higher trust level as well as into a more efficient working relationship. For example, a German supervisor reports how he had to become more flexible in order to support his Chinese subordinate, who in turn had to learn that communication in Germany is more straight forward than he is used to:

> *"He knows from me, when there is anything [...] well, let's say critical. Let's assume, well not legal but more in the sense of 'we have too many receivables', the customer owes us too much money. That I will not immediately cut him off. That kind of openness. And he in turn can meanwhile also say 'sorry, we will not solve the problem in two months.' While maybe one and a half years ago he would have said 'we will solve it until next week', knowing well though that this was impossible. Therefore I'd say everything is much more open now, and that has to do with trust." [tr]*

This example illustrates how both partners of a dyad learned to cope with their partner's expectations and consequently adapted to them, although they seemed alien in the light of their own culture. Trust emerged iteratively, by realizing the partner acts supportively, and finally translated into a higher quality of LMX.

It is thus shown, that while differing expectations in the beginning hinder the development of LMX, they can gradually be overcome by a mutual learning process. It is proposed that:

Proposition 2a: Chinese and Germans have different expectations in their respective supervisors/subordinates. Therefore, trust is built up by differing criteria, which has a negative influence on LMX in the beginning of the working relationship.

Investigating further on the notion that trust is built up by differing criteria in a Chinese and in a German business context, two main hindrances to the emergence of trust particular to a cross-cultural context become evident. Differing cultures as well as differing languages are repeatedly mentioned by interviewees as difficulties in the improvement of work relationships. Both hindrances were already touched upon in the previous paragraph, but are now examined in depth.

Participants of this study frequently reported how the differing cultural backgrounds render certain behaviors of their co-workers alien to them. Cultural clashes were identified mainly in the broad areas of communication, the importance of relationships as well as in the flexible treatment of rules and decisions. In the worst case cultural clashes were directly interpreted as a lack of support and thus lead to a violation of trust.

The following situation a Chinese subordinate was faced with during an assignment in Germany provides a profound insight on how communication differs between Germany and China. When lost on a deserted country road the subordinate called some German colleagues, explaining the situation. As a member of a high-context culture (Hall, 1976), the employee expected them to come for help. However, being members of low-context cultures (ibid.), the German colleagues simply advised the Chinese team-member to continue to drive to the next cross-road and ask someone for directions. The subordinate reflects:

"I thought I was already very direct! (Laughter) I really said I have a problem, but then later I talked to my colleagues and colleagues said, 'yes, you should say I want you to pick me up!' So that's the difference! I think direct really, it's-, I think maybe for Germany direct means talk about the things to do. [...] For Chinese it's very seldom to say 'I want you to do something for me!' No. I said I have a problem. [...] the normal reaction is, you will do something."

An example of the differing status of especially work relationships is given by another Chinese subordinate who similarly spent time in Germany. He remarks that a personal relationship apart from work between colleagues as emphasized in China does hardly exist in Germany. As member of a collectivistic culture (Hofstede, 1980) he is amazed at the German custom to separate work related and private communication:

"They even have two cell phones! One is for their work and another one even nobody knows."

A German supervisor employed in China comments on the same subject:

"In many German areas it's like that, for example if you want to host an event in the evening and say 'come on, tonight we all have dinner together', half of the team will say 'yes, but tonight I'm busy with the pigeon fancier club, or the sports club or I play the trumpet, tonight is really bad. And besides I hang out with you guys all day long, in the evening I want to be left

alone.' That's impossible in China. If you do something like that in China, everyone will show. And those who do not will apologize three times to the team and five times to their supervisor explaining why they can't make it on that particular day." [tr]

Finally, it was frequently remarked that rules and decisions are flexible and open to interpretation in China. Whereas for Chinese employees this circumstance is remarked as an asset, it gives German managers cause to despair. Accordingly, a Chinese manager describes:

"To be honest I experienced less Chinese bosses, but compared to the German thinking, they are really more flexible. [...] They can play today like this, but they can play like that tomorrow."

A German supervisor presents his view on the same circumstance as follows:

"It was really difficult for me and even today it is still not easy to accept that decisions that are made, are actually not fixed, they remain variable. [...] A new perspective is presented again and again so that as a German you really can give way to despair." [tr]

The different approach of Chinese and Germans towards rules and decisions can be explained with the marked difference of China and Germany in Hofstede's dimension of Uncertainty Avoidance. As adherence to rules as well as to made decisions reduces uncertainty (Hofstede, 2001, p. 160), Germans, different from Chinese, clearly prefer to abide by them (Brodbeck et al., 2002).

It is shown that the component of culture in cross-cultural dyads often leads to misunderstandings, typically in areas that are specific to one culture and thus alien to the member of the other culture. A Chinese interviewee summarizes:

"So right now this trust subject. The first problem, the German can't fully understand the Chinese idea. Chinese also can't fully understand the German idea, and the philosophy, culture and all the things behind this idea."

The finding coincides with the findings of Ren and Gray's (2009) work, namely that relationship conflicts emerge when one party of the cross-cultural LM-Dyad violates the other party's expectations about meeting one of his or her core needs

(Goffman, 1967, pp. 47) that are rooted in the respective culture. Such an action can constitute a breach of trust that subsequently needs to be restored.

However, interviewees reported further that not only the cultural differences constituted a challenge to the development of a trustful relationship. Without the topic being mentioned or hinted in the interview questions, nine out of 18 interviewees emphasized that the foreign language of their co-worker posed a substantial difficulty to the emergence of trust in their LM-Dyad. When asked whether the process of trust building was different with a Chinese than with a German, a German leader replied:

> *"Well, everyone was very confiding, very open, but then, until I really had the feeling for myself that trust had been built up - the first time until I had that feeling took a while [...]. What was probably also due to the English language." [tr]*

The language problem was also frequently mentioned in conjunction with the topic of expectations. Both, Germans and Chinese, leaders and members agree that language was a factor hindering the fulfillment of expectations. Exemplarily, a Chinese employee states:

> *"For example capacity, or competence or experience. So for this area some-times we cannot meet his expectations [...]. Because different people have a different level of competence. And for some the competencies it's not so easy to change. For example the language. In half a year, or one year, it's very hard."*

Since the fulfillment of expectations is again tied to trust as was shown in the previous paragraph, language clearly is a factor that has a negative impact on trust formation. This finding is congruent with Tenzer and colleagues' study (2014), who found that although diversity can have positive influences on MNTs, dif-fering languages yield exclusively negative effects on team work, mitigating the perceived trustworthiness of team members with limited language skills.

Both, differing cultural values and differing language constitute an obstacle to trust formation in cross-cultural LM-Dyads. However, these hindrances can be overcome by a change in the behavior of both co-workers. With only two explicit exceptions, the majority of interviewees stated that they changed their behavior towards their co-worker during the tenure of the working relationship in order to make it more efficient and consequently improve LMX. For example a German leader reflects:

> *"Well, we both did [change]. Maybe me less than him. Because as you utter many things simply the way they cross your mind in German, he couldn't understand everything immediately the way I meant it. So you have to slow down your speed or to explain the task visually [...], do things in English instead of German. Meaning you deploy language differently or use a different language to clarify something, yes, in that aspect I did change." [tr]*

Considering the initial difficulties in building up trust as described by the majority of interviewees, it is proposed:

Proposition 2b: Building trust is more difficult in a culturally diverse LM-Dyad than in a mono-cultural dyad, which has a negative influence on LMX.

Diversity research has identified both positive and negative effects of differing cultures on MNTs (Van Knippenberg & Schippers, 2007). Among defenders of the positive impact diversity exerts upon team work are Early and Mosakowski (2000), who find that cultural diversity can enhance team performance, as well as Ely and Thomas (2001) who postulate that cultural diversity yields learning effects and improves access to foreign markets.

However, diversity studies did not focus on the vertical dyad as unit of research, but laid focus on MNTs consisting of members of multiple nationalities. This study wants to verify the findings of diversity research for the concrete case of German-Chinese LM-Dyads and draw conclusions on the impact of diversity on trust formation and LMX.

Both Chinese and German participants of this study reported that they are able to capitalize on their partner's cultural diversity. A German leader points out:

> *"At the same time I think that only with the differing backgrounds you can really be successful here, in such an environment. Because we do work in a German company in China. And it is necessary to balance the expectations*

of the Chinese customer and the engineer sitting in Germany, it is a cultural balancing act. And a such is only possible in an intercultural team." [tr]

When asked about the strengths of their working relationships, the cultural gap was thus often named as an asset. A Chinese leader describes how he can put his partner's German nationality to use:

"You [i.e. a German] talking with a supplier you're as a god. [...] This somehow makes you, working is much more easier because you have quite a lot of influencing power."

Several Germans on the other hand reported how they profit from their partner's cultural knowledge, especially in the area of communication.

"Well the Chinese employees, or towards members of different Chinese companies, personal relationships have a big impact. And it helps me when he [i.e. his Chinese subordinate] is moderating that, he tells me ok, we have to go there again, we have to talk about this and that a second time." [tr]

Many times German interviewees mentioned the possibility to rely on their partner's cultural knowledge as a source of trust formation. For example, when asked what makes a person trustworthy a German supervisor replies:

"That's something I really appreciate about her. There were two or three situations in which I as a German, where she approached me afterwards when I had made a German decision and she said to me: 'We Chinese, we are a little bit different. Maybe we should do that a little bit differently.' And I say ok, that was a trust generating measure, I say 'ok, if you think so.' Subsequently I always asked: 'Is that ok for Chinese people?' " [tr]

In line with Ely and Thomas' (2001) findings, it is shown that both members of German-Chinese LM-Dyads can profit from their cultural diversity. Moreover, the diverse cultural setting, that is the mixture of a German company in a Chinese environment, helps to establish trust and finally contributes to a more efficient exchange. It is thus proposed that:

Proposition 2c: The cross-cultural setting of a MNC exerts positive influence on LMX in culturally diverse LM-Dyads, because both members of the dyad can put their complimentary abilities to use, which creates trust.

It was shown in this paragraph that due to a different understanding of leadership and thus a differing interpretation of a leader's and a member's respective duties and responsibilities, cultural diversity in LM-Dyads gives rise to disparate expectations. As expectations are tied closely to the emergence of trust and thus a positive exchange between leaders and members, it can be concluded that differing cultures first constitute a hindrance to the development of high-quality LMX. However, it was found that a learning process occurs and that finally the cross-cultural setting in which the dyad operates contributes to mutual trust generation.

4.3   The Process of Cultural Convergence

Floyd (1999) argued early on that eastern and Western management practices converge along with the process of globalization, the increased deployment of expatriates, continuous FDI activities and the harmonization of standards. It was surprising to find however, that although interviewees were not explicitly asked for their views on cultural convergence, the topic kept being mentioned. Therefore, the final thematic bloc of findings will answer the last research question mentioned in Chapter 2.6, namely whether cultural differences are decreasing with the younger generation. Especially in conjunction with the expectations Chinese employees have in their German supervisors as well as in conjunction with the way culture influences the dyadic work relationships, the issue of cultural convergence was mentioned regularly. A German supervisor observes:

"I don't have the feeling that culture plays a very important role. But I believe it is a significant fact that [...] in China you have the lower scope, let's say under 35 and then what is above that. [...] That means he [i.e. the subordinate] is part of the younger generation in China who doesn't display the old patterns of behavior, the unquestioning obedience towards the boss and so on." [tr]

Although it is not possible to draw a line at a certain age, the pattern identified by this German supervisor is verified in the conversation with younger Chinese managers or Chinese managers with profound experience in the German cultural background. For example, concerning the cultural pattern of Guanxi a younger Chinese manager states:

> *"A lot of Chinese guys will want to build up a relationship on purpose. [...]*
> *For example during some festival he will give something directly to his up-*
> *per manager and indirectly to the upper managers' families and their relati-*
> *ves and so on. To be honest I don't like that kind of behavior so I don't want*
> *to do that, [...] I don't want to build up some trust on purpose for this."*

When asked in which aspect the relationship towards his supervisor could use improvement, another Chinese manager who can draw upon experiences with several German superiors replied unexpectedly:

> *"Better communication. Because [...] for Chinese, because we have diffe-*
> *rent culture, for communication we'll not, especially for the leader, someti-*
> *mes it's not so well communicated with subordinates because he thinks 'oh,*
> *I've decided, so we will do it, not that!' but for the German boss he usually*
> *will prediscuss with you, then common understanding."*

In this case the Chinese subordinate wishes his German boss to include him more into his decisions, because he already made prior experiences with the German participative leadership style and grew accustomed to it. A German supervisor explains:

> *"Well, it's like that, it is perceived as 'Germans lead different than Chi-*
> *nese'. And the majority of Chinese prefer, or feel more at ease with the*
> *German way."* [tr]

When asked for the expectations he felt his Chinese subordinates had in him, the same manager answers:

> *"My experience is that especially to German bosses in China the expectation*
> *is: 'Act different from the Chinese bosses!' "* [tr]

He further comments that the German leadership techniques which are perceived as positive in the Chinese surrounding, are oftentimes taken as model and implemented by Chinese subordinates in the dealing with their own staff. This way the German participative leadership approach slowly disseminates throughout the company.

However, appreciation of the German leadership model is not only found among Chinese subordinates who feel encouraged by the possibility of participation. A Chinese leader comments on the positive aspects of the working relationship towards his German subordinate:

"Another point is, he's a really open and proactive or aggressive guy. If even sometimes he says to me 'ok, sorry I disagree with you. Because what, what, what...' You know, this makes me very happy, because you know I understand Germany now. If you say 'yes', ok, you cannot get the respect, reasonable. [...] Even we say we, even respect each other, but it doesn't mean we can stop the by saying 'no'. This is not the right way. If something happened for your aspects you should say 'no' immediately. And to all the other guys, and 'yes' they say 'no', and of course if something happened or cannot meet his personal expectation, he will immediately point out and will expect the feedback."

Although the behavior of his German subordinate doesn't correspond with the way traditional Chinese employees enact their role, the Chinese leader appreciates the differences and views them as enhancing efficiency.

A German supervisor comments on the differences observed between subordinates with traditional Chinese behavior and a younger subordinate with more understanding and appreciation of the German management style:

"And he also discusses controversially with me, what I appreciate, what I really like, while the other two, well they always - they always inquire a lot about what I think. And actually I want to educate them to think for themselves and make their own decisions." [tr]

The statement illustrates that high-quality LMX can be built up with the younger subordinate while this seems to be more difficult with members of the older generation. It is therefore proposed that:

Proposition 3: Cultures continue to merge, which is why the negative effects of cultural distance on LMX decrease in importance with age.

It was found in this paragraph that cultural convergence along with the gradual convergence of leadership styles (Floyd, 1999) enhances the reciprocal understanding of culturally diverse LM-Dyads. However, Wang (2014) found, that although leadership styles slowly converge with globalization and the gradual alignment of cultural values, differences between German and Chinese management practices remain visible and pronounced.

It is among the most important findings of this study, that German and Chinese cultures as well as management practices contain distinct features that render them unique. Although the differences often give rise to cultural clashes, they can also be put to use and thus contribute to a successful cross-border conduct of business.

5 Discussion

After presenting the findings of the conducted study, they are put into perspective by discussing them in the light of prior research in the following paragraph. The section will integrate the implications provided by the interviews with the theoretical background discussed in Chapter 2 in order to identify the study's contributions to existent theories. Furthermore the chapter will summarize the managerial implications of the findings as well as briefly discuss limitations of the study.

5.1 Theoretical Significance

The approach to LMX theory as well as to diversity research pursued in this study is unique in two distinct ways. By conducting semi-structured, in-depth interviews a qualitative method was applied, which is hardly found throughout LMX research. Furthermore, by taking the culturally diverse LM-Dyad as unit of data analysis an innovative angle on the theory was highlighted. The unique aspects of this study allow for the findings to contribute to LMX research in various ways.

First, as outlined in Chapter 3, it was among the initial aims of this study to take part in the long-needed and called-for consolidation of LMX theory. Schriesheim and colleagues (1999) criticized the lack of seminal theoretical papers that conceptualize and define the LMX construct, remarking that the partially blurred theory gave way for "an almost bewildering array" (Schriesheim et al., 1999, p. 63) of diverse LMX measures, dimensions and content. As the qualitative approach pursued in this study is not common throughout LMX research, the study design allows for more comprehensive research than was conducted in the past. It can thus add to LMX theory by extending on the conceptualization of the model by inductively building theory.

However, it is not the main intent of this study to consolidate and conceptualize LMX theory, but instead it aims at examining the effects of cultural diversity on trust and LMX. Therefore, the emergent findings contribute to LMX theory also in a second way, namely by adding the element of culture, more specifically the elements of German and Chinese culture with all their particularities. Taking the cross-cultural LM-Dyad as unit of data collection can thus contribute to LMX theory by deductively testing prior findings in a culturally diverse setting.

Finally, It was outlined in Chapter 3.2 that German management practices are underrepresented in English literature (Holden, 2008), whereas Chinese management practices are of special current interest to leadership theory due to the increasing economic importance of the country. The study's focus on Chinese and German management practices therefore also allows for contributions to culture-specific leadership theories.

Researchers are widely concordant that LMX and trust are positively related (e.g. Gómez & Rosen, 2001; Dirks & Ferrin, 2001; Brower et al., 2000). However, so far scholars couldn't agree upon the nature of the association (e.g. Scandura & Pelligrini, 2008), whether trust is is to be seen as an antecedent, a dimension, an outcome or a mere moderator variable acting on LMX. Although the findings derived in Chapter 4.1 cannot fully provide an answer to the debate, they still indicate that trust is neither an outcome of LMX nor a simple moderator variable. It was derived in proposition 1a, 1b and 1c, that trust clearly is to be seen as a precondition of high-quality LMX. Brower and colleagues (2000) furthermore point out, that Liden and Maslyn (1998) in their seminal work on the dimensionality of LMX asserted that the dimensions "contribute to the level of LMX in an additive fashion" (Liden & Maslyn, 1998, p. 235) thus also being interpretable as antecedents of the constructs. In connection with Brower and colleagues' understanding of the dimensionality of the LMX construct, it can be concluded according to the qualitative findings of this study, that trust is to be seen as antecedent of LMX, thus contributing to earlier findings of LMX theory.

Moreover it is the aim of this study to introduce the element of culture to LMX literature. It could be shown that the positive correlation of trust and LMX identified in literature (e.g. Gómez & Rosen, 2001; Dirks & Ferrin, 2001; Brower et al., 2000) also holds true in a cross-cultural context. Going one step further, this study finds that trust is of even greater importance in a culturally diverse LM-Dyad than in a mono-cultural LM-Dyad as trust can compensate for a lack of cultural knowledge or language skills. Theoretical knowledge is thus inductively extended for the importance of trust in culturally diverse LM-Dyads.

It was examined furthermore, whether trust plays an equally important role to members of both, the Chinese and the German cultural context. Contributing to Chinese and German management literature, it was found that trust is important for the establishment of high-quality LMX in both cultures.

However, in line with trust and management research (e.g. Johnson & Cullen, 2002; Law et al., 2000) the study revealed that the traditional concept of Guanxi is still prevalent in China and guides the rules of social exchange. Consequently, Chinese employees value trust less as compared to German employees, since they can reach the ultimate goal, that is a positive work outcome, also through informal ties and relationships with their superiors. It is important to know however, that Guanxi is not established in the same slow iterative fashion in which trust is built up (Mayer et al., 1995), but can also be existent through external factors that cannot be influenced by the persons themselves, such as being born in the same hometown, possessing the same last name or being classmates (Farh et al., 1998). This finding clearly contrasts the different importance Chinese and Germans place on the formation of high-quality LMX and is thus contributing to the field of LMX literature, indicating that the importance of LMX varies across cultures. The finding is consistent with Hofstede's (1993) study about cultural constraints in management theories, in which he questions the validity of Western management concepts in differing cultural contexts early on.

Diving deeper into the cultural differences specific to Germany and China, the study furthermore examined by which criteria trust is built up in both cultures respectively. In doing so, the means of qualitative research allowed for inductively deriving factors that influence the trust-building process in German-Chinese LM-Dyads. In line with literature, it was found that expectations substantially influence the process of trust generation (Colquitt et al., 2007). Evoked by differing leadership theories, both Germans and Chinese bring specific images of the role of an ideal, trustworthy supervisor as well as of an ideal, trustworthy subordinate with them. In accordance with research on paternalistic leadership as prevalent in China (Zhang et al., 2015) the study found that from a Chinese perspective an ideal leader is assertive, supportive and knowledgeable, whereas the ideal subordinate is loyal, supportive and diligent. In a German mindset, the prevalent participative leadership model coins the roles of supervisors and subordinates (Szabo et al., 2002), and in line with research it was found that the ideal German supervisor gives his subordinates insight into his decisions and lets them operate independently. The ideal German subordinate on the other hand is proactive, participative, voices his thoughts and works independently. The findings are also congruent with the concept of the German Dignity Culture and the Chinese Face Culture as described by Leung and Cohen (2011). In a Dignity Culture, relationships are marked by fair exchange and equality, whereas in a Face Culture hierarchies are emphasized. It was found furthermore, that the differing expectations clash frequently and thus negatively influence the trust-building process and also the process of establishing high-quality LMX. This finding yields further insights into LMX theory, contributing to the cross-cultural angle and shedding light on the trust-building process in German-Chinese LM-Dyads.

Agreeing with diversity scholars, next to a differing understanding of leadership, hindrances to the development of trustful work relationships were inductively identified in specific cultural values (e.g. Fukuyama, 1995; Doney et al., 1998) as well as in the lack of a common language (e.g. Tenzer et al., 2014). With regard to culture, the main impeding differences for the establishment of trustful work relationships between Chinese and Germans lay in the areas of communication, the valuation of work relationships as well as in the attitude towards rules and made decisions. Hindrances to trust formation were derived inductively and further contribute to culture specific management theories. Furthermore it was found, that the hindrances to trust formation also hinder the development of high-quality LMX, thereby extending on LMX theory.

As all interviewees were employed in either a Chinese subsidiary or a Joint Venture of a German MNE operating in Mainland China, the study found that the cross-cultural environment influences the exchange relationship of leaders and members. Ely and Thomas (2001) suggested that cultural diversity yields both positive and negative work outcomes for MNTs, listing learning effects and improved access to foreign markets among the positive effects of cultural diversity. Although their study was conducted in a purely US-American setting, their results are confirmed by the present study for German-Chinese LM-Dyads. Learning effects could be observed on both sides, and interviewees confirmed that the interaction of both nationalities yielded better results on the focal markets. The study hereby extended on diversity research for the concrete examples of China and Germany. As the influence of a cross-cultural surrounding on LMX has so far not been addressed, the study also contributed further to the body of research in LMX theory.

Finally it was derived from the data, that the ongoing, worldwide process of cultural approximation (House et al., 2002) as well as approximation of western and eastern management practices (Floyd, 1999) is noticeable in the cross-cultural setting of MNEs and fosters the development of high-quality LMX between leaders and members of German-Chinese LM-Dyads. As LMX research has so far not dealt with culturally diverse LM-Dyads, the finding has not been recognized in the body of LMX literature. It therefor extends upon the theory and points out the need for further investigation of culturally diverse LM-Dyads.

The conducted study is among the first to deal with culturally diverse LM-Dyads in the context of LMX theory. Its findings therefore add to the body of LMX literature. By investigating upon German-Chinese LM-Dyads, thereby taking a closer look at the cultural backgrounds of China and Germany, the study contributes furthermore to the specific leadership and management theories of these countries.

5.2 Managerial Implications

Practical implications of this study are mainly addressed to either Germans or Chinese who have a supervisor or a subordinate of the respective other culture. However, German expatriates to China as well as Chinese expatriates working in Germany can also profit from the insights derived in this work.

First and foremost the study emphasizes the importance of building up a trustful relationship among culturally diverse co-workers in order to achieve high-quality LMX and thus also an efficient working relationship that is marked by positive work outcomes. However, the study also finds that hindrances to building up a trusting relationship exist and that they are rooted in cultural and linguistic differences eminent to the differing cultural-national backgrounds. Managers who need to deal closely with members of the respective other culture are thus well advised to pay attention to cultural particularities in their co-worker's mindset.

Cultural values particular to China and Germany that provide potential to clash are identified in the areas of communication, valuation of relationships and respect of rules and decisions. Whereas Chinese are members of high-context Shame Cultures and thus derive meaning also from the context of a speech, Germans as members of low-context Dignity Cultures point out their thoughts directly. In order to avoid cultural clashes in the area of communication, both Germans and Chinese thus have to learn to pay attention to the particularities of the partner's style of communication, not only in order not to be understood, but much more in order to correctly interpret their partner's intentions. Secondly, relationships are valued higher in China as a collectivistic culture than in the German individualist culture. Team building activities are consequently an important part of work life in China, but not in Germany, a fact that needs to be taken into consideration when dealing with a colleague from the respective other culture. Finally, as a culture high in the dimension of Uncertainty Avoidance, Germans value rules and agreements, whereas Chinese, stemming from a culture low in Uncertainty Avoidance are more pragmatic and thus pursue a more flexible approach to dealing with rules.

Moreover it is found that differing cultural values yield a different understanding of leadership, as well as of the roles of superiors and subordinates. Different expectations in those roles lead to additional hindrances to the emergence of trust and high-quality LMX. Whereas Chinese employees expect a leader to be assertive, supportive and knowledgeable, Germans expect them to integrate subordinates in their decisions and to grant them independence. The ideal subordinate for a Chinese is loyal, supportive and diligent whereas for a German mindset he is proactive, participative, voices his thoughts and works independently. Quality of work is valued high in Germany, whereas in China quantity seems to be more important.

Managers of both sides need to render themselves conscious of the different expectations and cultural values of their co-workers, not primarily in order to avoid being rude but in order to understand their partner's behavior and thus building up trust and efficient working relationships.

With regard to language as a hindrance for the development of trust and high-quality LMX, managers are advised to consider potential errors in translation and thus need to verify whether their partner has understood critical points or not. Explanations can also be transported via sketches or the application of an easy language.

Furthermore, the study found that a partner's cultural knowledge can be used to the advantage of both parties when dealing with the respective foreign surrounding such as customers, consumers, suppliers, fellow employees or company structures. Managers should thus try to capitalize on their cultural diversity and deploy it specifically to reach common goals. This in turn helps to gradually build up trust and improve LMX (Möllering & Stache, 2010).

It is found that trust is a foundation of high-quality LMX and likewise for efficient work relationships. Building trust across cultures is thus one of the most important tasks in MNTs that should be accomplished in order to yield positive work outcomes.

5.3   Limitations

Although the study yields interesting insights to LMX theory, certain limitations that give way to further research have to be noticed. The most obvious among them is the limited number of participants due to which the number of conducted interviews was not sufficient to reach the point of data saturation (Locke, 2001, p. 53). Further interviews may thus have yielded additional or complementary findings that could have changed the direction of research or influenced the interpretation of data.

Furthermore, a bias can be observed in the selection of LM-Dyads. In the selection process of participants usually just one co-worker was approached initially. He or she then introduced one of his co-workers and asked him or her to participate in the study along with him. Interviewees were both informed about the interest of research before agreeing to being interviewed. As became obvious in the course of data collection, usually the first co-worker introduced a person that he or she had a very good and trustful relationship with already, or that stood out by an especially good performance. The average interviewed LM-Dyad was thus marked by high-quality LMX which may ultimately bias the findings. However, it is to be stated that the interviewed LM-Dyads had built up their trust and high-quality LMX over a longer period of time, and could thus also report of difficulties they had and how they overcame them.

In qualitative studies, the Hawthorne effect, which refers to the effect of being studied on a participant, has to be taken into account (Bryman & Bell, 2011, p. 58). As interviewed participants realize that they are being observed they may not respond naturally but instead bias their answers in order to appear in a more favorable light. This may be all the more true when talking about a close colleague. However, participants were assured that their answers remain anonymous, and most shared both, positive and negative experiences very openly, why it is assumed that although present, the effect did not significantly bias respondents' answers.

Finally, it is a clear limitation of this study that a cross-sectional study design was applied. Since no longitudinal examination of data was conducted, the development of trust and LMX in a culturally diverse LM-Dyad could not be observed. However, it can be countered that LM-Dyads with tenures spanning from six months to four years were interviewed and thus the dynamics of the development process of trust and LMX captured over time.

6   Conclusion

Using a qualitative approach, this study examined the process of high-quality LMX development in culturally diverse LM-Dyads, thereby taking special interest in the role of trust. Nine German-Chinese LM-Dyads have been questioned and results contribute to the body of LMX literature as well as to culture specific management and leadership theories.

Finding that trust is a prerequisite for efficient, high-quality LMX especially in culturally diverse LM-Dyads, the study encourages further research on LMX in cross-cultural LM-Dyads. It is hereby of particular interest, that the LMX construct is subject to cultural particularities, which is why LMX scholars need to further investigate the construct in the light of specific cultural backgrounds, in order to address the increased need to manage successfully across borders. Moreover, it was found that cultural differences and language barriers easily and frequently lead to misunderstandings, culture clashes and differing expectations of leaders and members in their respective co-worker. These cultural differences pose hindrances to the formation of a trustful work relationship and thus also the development of high-quality LMX that yields positive work outcomes. However, findings indicate that cultural diversity does not solely have negative outcomes on work relationships, but that instead co-workers can capitalize on the cultural diversity of their partners, after having established a trustful relationship. Finally it was found that along with the worldwide process of cultural approximation, trustful work relationships marked by high-quality exchange are established more easily within the younger generation, where cultural barriers are lower.

As the study is among the first to closely examine exchange processes in culturally diverse LM-Dyads, various promising areas for further research can be identified. Next to investigating LMX in the light of different specific cultural backgrounds, a longitudinal study examining the development of trust and high-quality LMX over time can yield further insights into the relationship dynamics of culturally diverse LM-Dyads. Research furthermore needs to continue broadening the conceptual base of LMX by qualitatively investigating upon the construct in a culturally diverse setting. However, by finding that without trust it is not possible to establish high-quality LMX across cultures, this study can serve as starting point for others, who set out to exploring LMX in the light of a cross-cultural background.

V References

Auerbach, C.F. & Silverstein, L.B., 2003. Qualitative Data: An Introduction to Coding and Analysis. New York: New York University Press.

Anand, S., Hu, J., Liden, R.C. & Vidyarthi, P. R., 2011. Leader–Member Exchange: Recent Research Findings and Prospects for the Future. In: Bryman, A., Collinson, D., Grint, K., Jackson, B. & Uhl-Bien, M., Eds., 2011. Sage Handbook of Leadership. Thousand Oaks: Sage Publications, pp. 311–325.

Aryee, S. & Chen, Z.X., 2006. Leader-Member Exchange in a Chinese Context: Antecedents, the Mediating Role of Psychological Empowerment and Outcomes. Journal of Business Research, 59(7), pp. 793-801.

Ayers, E., 1984. Vengeance and Justice. New York: Oxford University Press.

Bingham, C.B., Felin, T. & Black, J.S., 2000. An Interview With John Pepper: What it Takes to be a Global Leader. Human Resource Management, 39(2/3), pp. 287-292.

Birkinshaw, J., Brannen, M.Y., & Tung, R.L., 2011. From a Distance and Generalizable to up Close and Grounded: Reclaiming a Place for Qualitative Methods in International Business Research. Journal of International Business Studies, pp. 573-581.

Blau, P.M., 1964. Exchange and Power in Social Life. New York: John Wiley.

Brodbeck, F.C., Frese, M. & Javidan, M., 2002. Leadership Made in Germany: Low on Compassion, high on Performance. Academy of Management Executive, 16(1), pp. 16-29.

Brower, H.H., Lester, S.W., Korsgaard, M.A., & Dineen, B.R., 2009. A Closer Look at Trust Between Managers and Subordinates: Understanding the Effects of Both Trusting and Being Trusted on Subordinate Outcomes. Journal Of Management, 35(2), pp. 327-347.

Brower, H.H., Schoorman, F.D. & Tan, Hwee Hoon, 2000. A Model of Relational Leadership: The Integration of Trust and Leader-Member Exchange. Leadership Quarterly, 11(2), pp. 227-250.

Bryman, A. & Bell, E. 2011. Business Research Methods. 3rd ed. Oxford: Oxford University Press.

Castells, M., 2000. The Rise of the Network Society: The Information Age: Economy, Society and Culture. Vol. I, 2nd ed. Cambridge: Blackwell.

Colquitt, J.A., Scott, B.A. & LePine, J.A., 2007. Trust, Trustworthiness, and Trust Propensity: A Meta-Analytic Test of their Unique Relationships with Risk Taking and Job Performance. Journal of Applied Psychology, 92(4), pp. 909-927.

Chang, E. & Taylor, M.S., 1999. Control in Multinational Corporations (MNCs): The Case of Korean Manufacturing Subsidiaries. Journal of Management, 25(4), pp. 541-565.

Chen, C.C., Chen, X.-P. & Meindl, J.R., 1998. How Can Cooperation be Fostered? The Cultural Effects of Individualism-Collectivism. Academy of Management Review, 23(2), pp. 285–304.

Cheng, B.S., Chou, L.F., Wu, T.Y., Huang, M.P., & Farh, J. L., 2004. Paternalistic Leadership and Subordinate Responses: Establishing a Leadership Model in Chinese Organizations. Asian Journal of Social Psychology, 7(1), pp. 89-117.

Cheng, C., Jiang, D., Cheng, B., Riley, J. & Jen, C., 2015. When do Subordinates Commit to Their Supervisors? Different Effects of Perceived Supervisor Integrity and Support on Chinese and American Employees. Leadership Quarterly, 26(1), pp. 81-97.

Child, J. & Möllering, G., 2003. Contextual Confidence and Active Trust Development in the Chinese Business Environment. Organizations Science, 14(1), pp. 69-80.

Coleman, J.S., 1990. Foundations of Social Theory. Cambridge: Belknap Press.

Cropanzano, R. & Mitchell, M.S., 2005. Social Exchange Theory: An Interdisciplinary Review. Journal of Management, 31(6), pp. 874-900.

Cullen, J.B., Parbotheeah, K.P., 2014. Multinational Management: A Strategic Approach. 6th ed. Cincinnati: Southwestern University Press.

Dansereau, F., Graen, G. & Haga, W.J., 1975. A Vertical Dyad Linkage Approach to Leadership within Formal Organizations. Organizational Behavior and Human Performance, 13, pp. 46-78.

Dansereau, F., Cashman, J. & Graen, G., 1973. Instrumentality Theory and Equity Theory as Complementary Approaches in Predicting the Relationship of Leadership and Turnover among Managers. Organizational Behavior and Human Performance, 10(2), pp. 184-200.

Dienesch, R.M. & Liden, R.C., 1986. Leader-Member Exchange Model of Leadership: A Critique and Further Development. Academy of Management Review, 11(3), pp. 618-634.

Dietz, G., Gillespie, N. & Chao, G.T., 2010. Unraveling the Complexities of Trust and Culture. In: Saunders, M.N.K., Skinner, D., Dietz, G., Gillespie, N. & Lewicki, R.J., 2010: Organizational Trust: A Cultural Perspective. Cambridge: Cambridge University Press, pp. 3-41.

Dirks, K.T. & Ferrin, D.L., 2001. The Role of Trust in Organizational Settings. Organizational Science, 12(4), pp. 450-467.

Doney, P.M., Cannon, J.P. & Mullen, M.R., 1998. Understanding the Influence of National Culture on the Development of Trust. Academy of Management Review, 23(3), pp. 601-620.

Dresing, T. & Pehl, T., 2012. Praxisbuch Interview & Transkription – Regelsysteme und Anleitungen für qualitative ForscherInnen. 4th ed. Marburg: Eigenverlag Dr. Thorsten Dresing, Thorsten Pehl.

Dulebohn, J.H., Bommer, W.H., Liden, R.C., Brouer, R.L. & Ferris, G.R., 2012. A Meta-Analysis of Antecedents and Consequences of Leader-Member

Exchange: Integrating the Past With an Eye Toward the Future. Journal of Management, 38(6), pp. 1715-1759.

Duncan, P. & Herrera, R., 2014. The Relationship Between Diversity and the Multidimensional Measure of Leader-Member Exchange (LMX-MDM). Journal of Management Policy and Practice, 15(1), pp. 11-24.

Earley, P.C., & Mosakowski, E., 2000. Creating Hybrid Team Cultures: An Empirical Test of Transnational Team Functioning. Academy of Management Journal, 43(1), pp. 26-49.

Easterby-Smith. M., Malina. D. & Lu. Y., 1995. How Culture-Sensitive is HRM? A Comparative Analysis of Practice in Chinese and UK Companies. International Journal of Human Resource Management, 6(1), pp. 31-59.

Ely, R.J. & Thomas, D.A., 2001. Cultural Diversity at Work: The Effects of Diversity Perspectives on Work Group Processes and Outcomes. Administrative Science Quarterly, 46(2), pp. 229-273.

Erdogan, B. & Liden, R.C., 2006. Collectivism as a Moderator or Responses to Organizational Justice: Implications for Leader-Member Exchange and Integration. Journal of Organizational Behavior, 27(1), pp. 1-17.

Eriksson, P. & Kovalainen, A., 2008. Qualitative Methods in Business Research. Thousand Oaks: Sage Publications.

Eurostat, 2015. Database. [Online] Available at: http://appsso.eurostat.ec.europa.eu/nui/submitViewTableAction.do [Accessed October 1st 2015]

Farh, J.L. & Cheng, B.S., 2000. A Cultural Analysis of Paternalistic Leadership in Chinese Organizations. In: Li, J.T., Tsui, A.S. & Weldon, E., Eds., 2000. Management and Organizations in the Chinese Context. London: Macmillan, pp. 94-127.

Farh, J., Tsui, A.S., Xin, K. & Cheng, B., 1998. The Influence of Relational Demography and Guanxi: The Chinese Case. Organization Science, 9(4), pp. 471-488.

Federal Statistical Office (Statistisches Bundesamt), 2014. Foreign Trade. Ranking of Germany's Trading Partners in Foreign Trade. [Online] Available at: https://www.destatis.de/EN/FactsFigures/ NationalEconomyEnvironment/ForeignTrade/TradingPartners/Tables/ OrderRankGermanyTradingPartners.pdf?__blob=publicationFile [Accessed May 2nd 2015].

Ferrin, D.L. & Gillespie, N., 2010. Trust Differences Across National - Societal Cultures: Much to do, or Much ado About Nothing? In: Saunders, M.N.K., Skinner, D., Dietz, G., Gillespie, N. & Lewicki, R.J., 2010: Organizational Trust: A Cultural Perspective. Cambridge: Cambridge University Press, pp. 42-87.

Ferris, G.R., Liden, R.C., Munyon, T.P., Summers, J.K., Basik, K.J. & Buckley, M.R., 2009. Relationships at Work: Toward a Multidimensional Conceptualization of Dyadic Work Relationships. Journal of Management, 35(6), pp. 1379-1403.

Floyd, D., 1999. Eastern and Western Management Practices: Myth or Reality? Management Decision, 37(8), pp. 628-632.

Fukuyama, F., 1995. Trust: The Social Virtues and the Creation of Prosperity. New York: The Free Press.

Gerstner, C.R. & Day, D.V., 1997. Meta-Analytic Review of Leader-Member Exchange Theory: Correlates and Construct Issues. Journal of Applied Psychology, 82(6), pp. 827-844.

Goffman, E., 1967. Interaction Ritual. Essays on Face-to-Face Bahavior. New York: Anchor Books.

Gouldner, A.W., 1960. The Norm of Reciprocity: A Preliminary Statement. American Sociological Review, 25(2), pp. 161-177.

Gómez, C. & Rosen, B., 2001. The Leader-Member Exchange as a Link between Managerial Trust and Employee Empowerment. Group & Organization Management, 26(1), pp. 53-69.

Graen, G. & Cashman, J., 1975. A Role-Making Model of Leadership in Formal Organizations: A Development Approach. In: Hunt, J.G. & Larson, L.L., 1975. Leadership Frontiers. Kent: Kent State University Press, pp. 143-165.

Graen, G., Cashman, J., Ginsburg, S. & Schiemann, W., 1977. Effects of Linking-Pin Quality on the Quality of Working Life of Lower Participants. Administrative Science Quarterly, 22(3), pp. 491-504.

Graen, G. Dansereau, F. & Minami, T., 1972. Dysfunctional leadership styles. Organizational Behavior and Human Performance, 7(2), pp. 216-236.

Graen, G., Novak, M. & Sommerkamp, P., 1982. The Effects of Leader-Member Exchange and Job Design on Productivity and Satisfaction: Testing a Dual Attachment Model. Organizational Behavior and Human Performance, 30(1), pp. 109-131.

Graen, G. & Scandura, T.A., 1987. Toward a Psychology of Dyadic Organizing. Research in Organizational Behavior, 9, pp. 175-208.

Graen, G. & Uhl-Bien, M., 1991. The Transformation of Professionals Into Self-Managing and Partially Self-Designing Contributors: Toward a Theory of Leadership-Making. Journal of Management Systems, 3(3), pp. 25-39.

Greguras, G.J., Ford, J.M. 2006. An examination of the Multidimensionality of Supervisor and Subordinate Perceptions of Leader-Member Exchange. Journal of Occupational & Organizational Psychology, 79(3), pp. 433-465.

Hall, E.T., 1976. Beyond Culture. New York: Anchor Books.

Heine, S.J., 2001. Self as Cultural Product: An Examination of East Asian and North American Selves. Journal of Personality, 69(6), pp. 881-906.

Hemesath, M. & Pomponio, X., 1998. Cooperation and Culture: Students From China and the United States in a Prisoner's Dilemma. Cross-Cultural Research, 32(2), pp. 171-184.

Heyer-Young, V., 2005. Ruth Benedict: Beyond Relativity, Beyond Pattern. Lincoln: University of Nebraska Press.

Hiller, N.J. & Day, D.D., 2003. LMX and Teamwork: The Challenges and Opportunities of Diversity. In: Graen, G.B. ed., 2003. Dealing with Diversity. Greenwich: Information Age Publishing, pp. 29-57.

Hofstede, G., 1993. Cultural Constraints in Management Theories. Academy of Management Executive, 7(1), pp. 81-94.

Hofstede, G., 1980. Culture's Consequences: International Differences in Work-Related Values. Newbury Park: Sage Publications.

Hofstede, G., 2001. Culture's Consequences. Comparing Values, Behaviors, Institutions and Organizations Across Nations. 2nd ed. Thousand Oaks: Sage Publications.

Holden, N., 2008. Reflections of a Cross-Cultural Scholar. Context and Language in Management Thought. International Journal of Cross Cultural Management, 8(2), pp. 239-251.

House, R.J., Hanges, P.J., Javidan, M., Dorfman, P.W., & Gupta, V., 2004. Culture, Leadership, and Organizations: The GLOBE Study of 62 Societies. Thousand Oaks: Sage Publications.

Hout, T., & Michael, D., 2014. A Chinese Approach to Management. Harvard Business Review, 92(9), pp. 103-107.

Hosmer, L.T., 1995. Trust: The Connecting Link Between Organizational Theory and Philosophical Ethics. Academy of Management Review, 20(2), pp. 379-403.

IMF - International Monetary Fund, 2015. World Economic Outlook Database. [Online] Available at: http://www.imf.org/external/pubs/ft/weo/2015/01/weodata/weorept.aspx?sy=20 00&ey=2020&scsm=1&ssd=1&sort=country&ds=.&br=1&pr1.x=32&pr1.y=10&c=213%2C124%2C156%2C228%2C924%2C128%2C134%2C466%2C111&s=NGDPD%2CNGDPDPC%2CNG

AP_NPGDP%2CPPPGDP%2CPPPPC%2CPPPSH%2CTX_RPCH&grp
=0&a=#download [Accessed May 1st, 2015].

Itim International, 2015. The Hofstede Centre. Strategy, Culture, Change.
[Online] Available at: http://geert-hofstede.com/china.html [Accessed May
2nd, 2015].

Javidan, M., Dorfman, P.W., De Luque, M.S., & House, R.J., 2006. In the
Eye of the Beholder: Cross Cultural Lessons in Leadership From Project
GLOBE. Academy of Management Perspectives, 20(1), pp. 67-90.

Johnson, J.L. & Cullen, J.B., 2002. Trust in Cross-Cultural Relationships. In:
Gannon, M.J. & Newman, K.L., 2002. The Blackwell Handbook of Cross-
Cultural Management. Oxford: Blackwell Publishers Ltd., pp. 335-360.

Kim, Y.-H. & Son, J., 1998. Trust, Cooperation and Social Risk: A Cross-
Cultural Comparison. Korea Journal, 38(1), pp. 131-143.

Kluckhohn, F.R. & Strodtbeck, F.L., 1961. Variations in Value Orientations.
Evanston: Row, Peterson.

Kuckartz, U., Dresing, T., Rädiker, S. & Stefer, C., 2008. Qualitative
Evaluation - Der Einstieg in die Praxis. 2nd ed. Wiesbaden: VS Verlag für
Sozialwissenschaften.

Lane, C., 1998. Introduction: Theories and Issues in the Study of Trust.
In: Lane, C. & Bachmann, R., Eds., 1998. Trust Within and Between
Organizations. Oxford: Oxford University Press, pp. 1-30.

Lane, C., 1997. The Social Regulation of Inter-Firm Relations in Britain and
Germany: Market Rules, Legal Norms and Technical Standards. Cambridge
Journal of Economics, 21(2), pp. 197-215.

Lane, C. & Bachmann, R., 1997. Co-operation in Inter-Firm Relations in
Britain and in Germany: The Role of Social Institutions. The British Journal
of Sociology, 48(2), pp. 226-254.

Langenberg, E.A., 2007. Guanxi and Business Strategy. Theory and Implications for Multinational Companies in China. Heidelberg: Physica-Verlag.

Law, K.S., Wong, C.-S., Wang, D. & Wang, L., 2000. Effect of Supervisor-Subordinate Guanxi on Supervisory Decisions in China: An Empirical Investigation. International Journal of Human Resource Management, 11(4), pp. 751-765.

Leung, A.K.Y. & Cohen, D., 2011. Within- and Between-Culture Variation: Individual Differences and the Cultural Logics of Honor, Face, and Dignity Cultures. Journal of Personality and Social Psychology, 100(3), pp. 507–526.

Lewicki, R.J., & Bunker, B.B., 1995. Trust in Relationships: A Model of Trust Development and Decline. In: Bunker, B.B. & Rubin, J.Z., Eds., 1995. Conflict, Cooperation, and Justice, San Francisco, CA: Jossey-Bass, pp. 133- 173.

Lewicki, R.J., McAllister, D.J. & Bies, R.J., 1998. Trust and Distrust: New Relationships and Realities. Academy of Management Review, 23(3), pp. 438-458.

Li, S., 2013. China's (Painful) Transition from Relation-Based to Rule-Based Governance: When and How, Not If and Why. Corporate Governance: An International Review, 21(6), pp. 567-576.

Liden, R.C. & Maslyn, J.M., 1998. Multidimensionality of Leader-Member Exchange: An Empirical Assessment through Scale Development. Journal of Management, 24(1), pp. 43-72.

Liden, R.C., Sparrowe, R.T., & Wayne, S.J., 1997. Leader-Member Exchange Theory: The Past and Potential for the Future. In: Ferris, G.R. Ed., 1997. Research in Personal and Human Resources Management, 15, Greenwich, CT: JAI Press, pp. 47–119.

Liden, R.C., Wayne, S.J. & Stilwell, D., 1993. A Longitudinal Study on the Early Development of Leader-Member Exchanges. Journal of Applied Psychology, 78(4), pp. 662-674.

Locke, K.D., 2001. Grounded Theory in Management Research. Thousand Oaks: Sage Publications.

Mantere, S. & Ketokivi, M., 2013. Reasoning in Organization Science. Academy of Management Review, 38(1), pp. 70-89.

Markus, H. & Kitayama, S., 1991. Culture and Self: Implications for Cognition, Emotion and Motivation. Psychological Review, 98 (2), pp. 224-253.

Mayer, R.C., Davis, J.H. & Schoorman, F.D., 1995. An Integrative Model of Organizational Trust. Academy of Management Review, 20(3), pp. 709-734.

McAllister, D.J., 1995. Affect- and Cognition-Based Trust as Foundations for Interpersonal Cooperation in Organizations. Academy of Management Journal, 38(1), pp. 24-59.

Mead, R. & Andrews, T.G., 2009. International Management. Chichester: John Wiley & Sons, Ltd.

Miles, R.E., & Creed, W.E., 1995. Organizational Forms and Managerial Philosophies: A Descriptive and Analytical Review. In: Staw, B.M. & Cummings, L.L., Eds., 1995. Research in Organizational Behavior. (Vol. 17). Greenwich: JAI Press, pp. 333-372.

Möllering, G. & Stache, F., 2010. Trust Development in German-Ukrainian Business Relationships. Dealing With Cultural Differences in an Uncertain Institutional Context. In: Saunders, M.N.K., Skinner, D., Dietz, G., Gillespie, N. & Lewicki, R.J., 2010: Organizational Trust: A Cultural Perspective. Cambridge: Cambridge University Press, pp. 205-226.

Morgan, G, & Smircich, L., 1980. The Case for Qualitative Research. Academy Of Management Review, 5(4), pp. 491-500.

Myers, M.D., 2008. Qualitative Research in Business and Management. Thousand Oaks: Sage Publications.

National Bureau of Statistics of China (中华人民共和国国家统计局), 2014. China Statistical Yearbook 2014. [Online] Available at: http://www.stats.gov. cn/tjsj/ndsj/2014/indexeh.htm [Accessed May 2nd, 2015].

Noorderhaven, N.G., 1999. National Culture and the Development of Trust: The Need for more Data and Less Theory. Academy of Management Review, 24(1), pp. 9-10.

Neeley, T.B., 2013. Language Matters: Status Loss and Achieved Status Distinction in Global Organizations. Organization Science, 24(2), pp. 476-497.

Niles, F.S., 1998. Individualism-Collectivism Revisited. Cross-Cultural Research, 32(4), pp. 315-341.

OECD - Organization for Economic Cooperation and Development (2014): OECD International Direct Investment Statistics.

Phillips, R.L., Duran, C.A. & Howell, R.D., 1993. An Examination of the Multidimensionality Hypothesis of Leader-Member Exchange, Using Both Factor Analytic and Structural Modeling Techniques. Proceedings of the Southern Management Association, pp. 161-163.

Pudelko, M., 2006. A Comparison of HRM Systems in the USA, Japan and Germany in their Socio-Economic Context. Human Resource Management Journal, 16(2), pp. 123-153.

Ren, H. & Gray, B., 2009. Repairing Relationship Conflict: How Violation Types and Culture Influence the Effectiveness of Restoration Rituals. Academy of Management Review, 34(1), pp. 105-126.

Rockstuhl, T., Dulebohn, J.H., Ang, S. & Shore, L.M., 2012. Leader-Member Exchange (LMX) and Culture: A Meta-Analysis of Correlates of LMX Across 2 Countries. Journal of Applied Psychology, 97(6), pp. 1097-1130.

Rousseau, D.M., Sitkin, S.B., Burt, R.S. & Camerer, C., 1998. Not so Different After All: A Cross-Discipline View of Trust. Academy of Management Review, 23(3), pp. 393-404.

Roth, K. & Kostova, T. 2003. The Use of the Multinational Corporation as a Research Context. Journal of Management, 29(6), pp. 883-902.

Rubin, H.J. & Rubin, I.S., 2012. Qualitative Interviewing – The Art of Hearing Data. 3rd ed. Thousand Oaks: Sage Publications.

Saunders, M.N.K., Skinner, D., Dietz, G., Gillespie, N. & Lewicki, R., Eds., 2010. Organizational Trust: A Cultural Perspective. Cambridge: Cambridge University Press.

Saunders, M., Lewis, P. & Thornhill, A., 2012. Research Methods for Business Students. 6th ed. Harlow: Pearson.

Scandura, T.A., Graen, G.B. & Novak, M.A., 1986. When Managers Decide Not to Decide Autocratically: An Investigation of Leader-Member Exchange and Decision Influence. Journal of Applied Psychology, 71(4), pp. 579-684.

Scandura, T.A. & Lankau, M.J., 1996. Developing Diverse Leaders: A Leader-Member Exchange Approach. Leadership Quarterly, 7(2), pp. 243-263.

Scandura, T.A. & Pelligrini, T.E., 2008. Trust and Leader-Member Exchange. A Closer Look at Relational Vulnerability. Journal of Leadership & Organizational Studies, 15(2), pp. 101-110.

Schaubroeck, J. & Lam, S.K., 2002. How Similarity to Peers and Supervisor Influences Organizational Advancement in Different Cultures. Academy of Management Journal, 45(6), pp. 1120-1136.

Schoorman, F.D., Mayer, R.C. & Davis, J.H., 2007. An Integrative Model of Organizational Trust: Past, Present, and Future. Academy of Management Review, 32(2), pp. 244-354.

Schriesheim, C.A., Castro, S.L. & Cogliser, C.C., 1999. Leader-Member Exchange (LMX) Research: A Comprehensive Review of Theory, Measurement, and Data-Analytic Practices. Leadership Quarterly, 10(1), pp. 63-113.

Schwartz, S.H.,1994. Are There Universal Aspects in the Structure and Contents of Human Values? Journal of Social Issues, 50(4), pp. 19-45.

Schyns, B., Paul, T., Mohr, G. & Blank, H., 2005. Comparing Antecedents and Consequences of Leader-Member Exchange in a German Working Context to Findings in the US. European Journal of Work and Organizational Psychology, 14(1), pp. 1-22.

Serva, M.A., Fuller, M.A. & Mayer, R.C., 2005. The Reciprocal Nature of Trust: A Longitudinal Study of Interacting Teams. Journal of Organizational Behavior, 26(6), pp. 625-648.

Settoon, R.P., Bennett, N., & Liden, R.C., 1996. Social Exchange in Organizations: Perceived Organizational Support, Leader-Member Exchange and Employee Reciprocity. Journal of Applied Psychology, 81(3), pp. 219-227.

Shaw, Z.H., 2009. The „One-Country, Two-System" Model and Its Applicability to Taiwan: A Study of Opinion Polls in Taiwan. Modern China Studies, 16(4), pp. 96-122.

Singelis, T.M., Triandis, H.C., Bhawuk, D.P.S. & Gelfand, M.J., 1995. Horizontal and Vertical Dimensions of Individualism and Collectivism: A Theoretical and Measurement Refinement. Cross Cultural Research, 29(3), pp. 240-275.

Sitkin, S.B., 1995. On the Positive Effect of Legalization on Trust. In: Bies, R.J., Lewicki, R.I. & Sheppard, B.H., Eds., 1995. Research on Negotiation in Organizations, (5), pp. 185-217. Greenwich: JAI Press.

Sitkin. S.B. & Roth, N.L., 1993. Explaining the Limited Effectiveness of Legalistic „Remedies" for Trust/Distrust. Organizational Science, 4(3), pp. 367-392.

So, A.Y., 2011. ‚One Country, Two Systems' and Hong Kong-China National Integration: A Crisis-Transformation Perspective. Journal Of Contemporary Asia, 41(1), pp. 99-116.

Stokes, P., & Wall, T., 2014. Research Methods. London: Palgrave.

Sullivan, D.M., Mitchell, M.S. & Uhl-Bien, M., 2003. The New Conduct of Business. How LMX Can Help Capitalize on Cultural Diversity. In: Graen, G.B. Ed., 2003. Dealing with Diversity. Greenwich: Information Age Publishing, pp. 183-218.

Szabo, E., Brodbeck, F.C., Den Hartog, D.N., Reber, G., Weibler, J., & Wunderer, R. 2002. The Germanic Europe Cluster: Where Employees Have a Voice. Journal Of World Business, 37(1), pp. 55-68.

Tenzer, H., Pudelko, M. & Harzing, A.W., 2014. The Impact of Language Barriers on Trust Formation in Multinational Teams. Journal of International Business Studies, 45(5), pp. 508-535.

Triandis, H.C., 1995. Individualism and Collectivism. Boulder: Westview Press.

Trompenaars, F., 1993. Riding the Waves of Culture: Understanding Cultural Diversity in Business. London: The Economist Books.

Trompenaars, F., & Hampden-Turner, C., 1997. Riding the Waves of Culture: Understanding Cultural Diversity in Business. 2nd ed. London: Nicholas Brealey Publishing.

Vanneste, B.S., Puranam, P. & Kretschmer, T., 2014. Trust Over Time in Exchange Relationships: Meta-Analysis and Theory. Strategic Management Journal, 35(12), pp. 1891-1902.

Van Knippenberg, D. & Schippers, M.C., 2007. Work Group Diversity. Annual Review of Psychology, 58, pp. 515-541.

Varma, A., Srinivas, E.S. & Stroh, L.K., 2005. A Comparative Study of the Impact of Leader-Member Exchange Relationships in the U.S. and India. Cross-Cultural Management: An International Journal, 12(1), pp. 84-95.

Wang, J., 2015. Globalization of Leadership Development. An Empirical Study of Impact on German and Chinese Managers. Wiesbaden: Springer Gabler.

Wayne, S.J., Shore, L.M. & Liden, R.C., 1997. Perceived Organizational Support and Leader-Member Exchange. A Social Exchange Perspective. Academy of Management Journal, 40(1), pp. 82-111.

Witzel, A. 2000. The Problem-Centered Interview. Forum: Qualitative Social Research, 1(1), Article 22. [Online] Available at: http://www.qualitative-research.net/index.php/fqs/article/view/1132/2522 [Accessed May 3rd, 2015].

World Population Statistics, 2014. Population of China 2014. [Online] Available at: http://www.worldpopulationstatistics.com/population-of-china-2014/ [Accessed May 1st, 2015].

World Values Survey, 2015. World Values Survey Wave 6. [Online]: Available at: http://www.worldvaluessurvey.org/WVSOnline.jsp [Accessed May 8th, 2015].

Wu, M., Huang, X., & Chan, S.H., 2012. The Influencing Mechanisms of Paternalistic Leadership in Mainland China. Asia Pacific Business Review, 18(4), pp. 631-648.

Zaheer, S. & Zaheer, A., 2006. Trust Across Borders. Journal of International Business Studies, 37(1), pp. 21-29.

Zhang, Y., Huai, M.-Y. & Xie, Y.-H., 2015. Paternalistic Leadership and Employee Voice in China: A Dual Process Model. The Leadership Quarterly, 26(1), pp. 25-36.

VI Appendix – Interview Outline

I. General Introduction
This section aims at getting to know the interviewee and his business background.

Please introduce yourself, including your age, nationality and gender.

Which company are you currently employed at and how long have you been working for this company?

What is the position you currently hold at this company and for how long have you been holding it? What are the main responsibilities coming along with it?

(G): For how long have you been working in China, and did you have any other China-related responsibilities before?

(Ch): For how long have you been employed at a foreign company? Have you had other experiences with a Western culture?

For how long have you been working together with your supervisor/subordinate?

For how long have you been knowing your supervisor/subordinate?

When you first met your supervisor/subordinate, was it in the respective positions you both currently occupy?

II. Expectations across Cultural Dimensions
This section aims at understanding different values and expectations of the members of differing cultural backgrounds. It is taken for granted that a Chinese co-worker is part of a vertical-collectivistic culture whereas a German co-worker is a member of a horizontal-individualistic culture.

What are your general expectations in a supervisor/subordinate?

It is often said that for example the personal component of a business relationship is valued higher in China than in Germany. Do you think that expectations in a supervisor/subordinate vary between the two cultures? Have you made any experiences with such different expectations?

In which aspects did your co-worker fulfill your expectations?

In which aspects did your co-worker NOT fulfill your expectations?

Did you observe a learning process in the (professional and private) behavior of your co-worker, so that he gradually met your expectations to a larger extent?

What do you think were your co-workers original expectations in you?

Do you have the feeling you could live up to his expectations from the beginning?

Did you change your own behavior towards your co-worker while working with him?

During the time you have worked together, did the image you had of your co-worker change?

III. Quality of LMX
This section shall examine the quality of the four dimensions of Leader-Member Exchange (Contribution, Loyalty, Professional Respect and Affect) to be able to deduct the outcome of Trust on LMX.

In which aspects do you think the working-relationship with your supervisor/subordinate is particularly strong?

What are the points where you think your working-relationship needs improvement?

In which aspects do you think that the different cultural background is influencing your working-relationship?

Did you develop ways to deal with those differences when they come up?

Do you consider that the quality of your working-relationship has changed over time? How?

IV. Dimensions of Trust

This section aims at examining which dimension of trust (calculus-based or identification-based) matters more to the interviewee and how it influenced their LMX at different stages.

Do you think trust is an important factor in your working-relationship? Why?

Building trust is always a critical step in a relationship. What helped you to build up trust with your supervisor/subordinate?

Was the trust-building process different than it would have been with someone from your own culture?

What are attributes that in your eyes make someone trustworthy? Do you think your supervisor/subordinate has different views on that?

In which respects do you consider your supervisor/subordinate to be trustworthy?

Along with the development of your relationship, did the level of trust you put in your co-worker change? How?

V. Fairness – Additional Section

China and Germany are very different when it comes to relationships with supervisors/subordinates, but also when it comes to fairness. Which differences could you detect from your personal experience or what you have perceived in your environment?

Do you think your supervisor/subordinate is fair? Do you have specific examples why you think he is fair? How did you react / give him in return.

How / in which respect did your fairness perceptions / concept change during the time you were working in China / with a person with a different background?

Do you think your organization is fair? Do you have specific examples why you think it is fair? How do you react to it?

Is the company culture here differently when it comes to fairness than in Germany?

XXX

VI. Business Ethics – Additional Section

Is there a different understanding of ethics in the working environment between Germany and China? What is it? Why do you think that there is a different understanding?

How do you cope with the different understanding?

Do you think your supervisor / subordinate is ethical (Chinese word is: 道德 dao de)? Why?
Did your understanding of ethical leadership change since you were working in China / (or for Chinese people: change since you were working in a German company).

Is the company ethical? Why?

Is there a different understanding of an ethical company or ethical working environment in Germany and in China? In which respect?
What do you do to make the organization atmosphere more ethical? Are there cultural aspects that you consider?

What is the difference between ethics and fairness?